AMERICA THROUGH EUROPEAN EYES

NOTES ON

A JOURNEY IN AMERICA

LETTERS FROM ILLINOIS

D1283494

NOTES

ON A

JOURNEY IN AMERICA

FROM THE

COAST OF VIRGINIA

TO THE

TERRITORY OF ILLINOIS

BY

MORRIS BIRKBECK *1764-1825*

TO WHICH IS ADDED

LETTERS FROM ILLINOIS

[1818]

AUGUSTUS M. KELLEY · PUBLISHERS

NEW YORK 1971

NOTES ON A JOURNEY IN AMERICA

First Edition 1818

Third Edition 1818

(London: *Printed by Severn & Co., 1 Skinner Street, Bishopsgate, for* James Ridgway, *Piccadilly*, 1818)

LETTERS FROM ILLINOIS

First Edition 1818

Third Edition 1818

(London: *Printed for* Taylor & Hessey, *93 Fleet Street*, 1818)

Reprinted 1971 by

AUGUSTUS M. KELLEY · PUBLISHERS

REPRINTS OF ECONOMIC CLASSICS

New York New York 10001

. . . .

I S B N 0 678 00686 5

L C N 71 119545

. . . .

PRINTED IN THE UNITED STATES OF AMERICA
by SENTRY PRESS, NEW YORK, N. Y. 10019

NOTES ON A JOURNEY IN AMERICA

NOTES

ON A

JOURNEY IN AMERICA,

FROM THE

COAST OF VIRGINIA

TO THE

TERRITORY OF ILLINOIS.

....

By *MORRIS BIRKBECK,*

Author of " Notes on a Tour in France."

....

THE THIRD EDITION.

....

London:

Printed by Severn & Co., 1, Skinner Street, Bishopsgate:

FOR JAMES RIDGWAY, PICCADILLY; AND TO BE
HAD OF ALL OTHER BOOKSELLERS.

———

1818.

Published by the same Author,

NOTES on a Journey through France, from Dieppe, through Paris and Lyons, to the Pyrennees, and back through Toulouse, in July, August, and September, 1814, describing the Habits of the People and the Agriculture of the Country. The 5th Edition. Price 4s. 6d.

TO MY ENGLISH FRIENDS.

I HAVE amused myself during our long, but by no means wearisome journey, by keeping this short record of occurrences and observations, of which *I* have now finished the revisal.

It contains just the particulars which *I* wish to communicate to my friends, written, *I* think, with as much simplicity of intention, as a private letter, but with a little more care, seeing *I* had the fear of the press before my eyes.

There are many for whom *I* entertain a sincere affection who have not received a line from me since our departure. *I* have always had more to say than a letter could contain; and now, instead of mutilated scraps, *I* beg they will accept this little book, and consider it as particularly addressed to them; for it certainly was composed most particularly for their information.

It may be collected from the tenor of these notes, that *I* am as well satisfied *with this country as I had anticipated;, and our friends will have sympathized with us in the success of our enterprise; having found a good country, and secured for ourselves a situation in it, so well adapted to our wishes: but, as friends are not used to gather each other's sentiments, on interesting topics by inference merely, they have a right to hear from me in direct terms, that my expectations and hopes are thus far more than satisfied with regard to the objects of our removal into this country.*

There are advantages before us greater than I had in contemplation; and apparently attainable with less difficulty and sacrifices. I have therefore nothing to regret in the step I have taken; and in my present knowledge I should find stronger motives for it.

M. B.

Sept. 1, 1817.

NOTES

ON A

JOURNEY IN AMERICA.

April 26, 1817—500 *Miles E. of Cape Henry,*
Virginia.

AFTER twelve months spent in the arrangement of my affairs I have embarked in comfort
with the greatest part of my family in quest of a
new settlement in the western wilderness.

We sailed on the 30th of March from Graves-
end, on board the good ship America, of 500
tons burthen, Captain Heth, for Richmond, Virginia. Our party occupies both the cabin and
steerage, excepting two strangers in the latter,
who are well-behaved, unobtrusive persons.

The captain is an agreeable and most friendly
man, and our accommodations are excellent: we
have had variety of winds and weather, but
mostly favourable: some of us have suffered from
sea-sickness, but we are now generally in good
health, and our spirits seem to partake of the
buoyancy of the noble vessel, which is convey-

ing us so cheerfully towards the place of our voluntary exile.

Having had the advantage of communicating with many respectable and well-informed Americans during this year of preparation, I have acquired some knowledge of the United States, as well as great store of introductory letters. A kind friend also put into my hands, just before our departure, a series of Geographical Works, lately published by Mr. Melish of Philadelphia. With the information derived from these and other sources, I feel qualified to enter with the more confidence on the task before me ; and I am in hopes that a journal of my proceedings may prove useful to others under similar circumstances, by way of warning or encouragement, as the event may prove of my own experience : and that my readers may accompany me with greater satisfaction and advantage, I shall premise something about myself, my motives, and plans, which will enable them to form a more just estimate of my opinions : I hope, however, in so doing, I shall not merit the imputation of egotism.

In the first place, being neither well able nor well disposed to combat the extremes of heat and cold which prevail to the east of the Alleghany mountains, I have pre-determined to pitch my tent to the westward of that ridge, and to the southward of Lake Erie, under a climate recommended by the concurrent testimony of all travellers, as temperate, salubrious and delightful.

Again,—Slavery, "that broadest, foulest blot," which still prevails over so large a portion of the United States, will circumscribe my choice within still narrower limits; for, if political liberty be so precious, that to obtain it, I can forego the well-earned comforts of an English home, it must not be to degrade myself and corrupt my children by the practice of slave-keeping.

This curse has taken fast hold of Kentucky, Tenessee, and all the new states to the south; therefore, my enquiries will be confined to the western part of Pennsylvania, and the states of Ohio, Indiana and the territory of Illinois: thus, in the immense field before us, the object of our search will be found, if found at all, within a comparatively narrow space.

To this main object I shall apply myself immediately, and deferring to a future opportunity the pleasure of travelling through the Atlantic States, I intend, on my arrival, to repair westward with all convenient speed, in order to take a deliberate survey of those western regions, with the hope of fixing on the place of our final settlement before the ensuing winter.

Before I enter on these new cares and toils, I must take a parting glance at those I have left behind ; and they are of a nature unhappily too familiar to a large proportion of my countrymen to require description.

How many are there, who, having capitals in business which would be equal to their support at simple interest, are submitting to privations under the name of economy, which are near a-kin to the sufferings of poverty ; and denying themselves the very comforts of life to escape taxation; and yet their difficulties increase, their capitals moulder away, and the resources fail on which they had relied for the future establishment of their families.

A nation, with half its population supported by alms, or poor-rates, and one fourth of its income derived from taxes, many of which are dried up in their sources, or speedily becoming so, must teem with emigrants from one end to the other : and, for such as myself, who have had " nothing to do with the laws but to obey them," it is quite reasonable and just to secure a timely retreat from the approaching crisis— either of anarchy or despotism.

An English farmer, to which class I had the honour to belong, is in possession of the same rights and privileges with the *Villeins* of old time, and exhibits for the most part, a suitable

political charater. He has no voice in the appointment of the legislature unless he happen to
possess a freehold of forty shillings a year, and
he is then expected to vote in the interest of his
landlord. He has no concern with public affairs excepting as a tax-payer, a parish officer,
or a militia man. He has no right to appear at
a county meeting, unless the word *inhabitant*
should find its way into the sheriff's invitation :
in this case he may shew his face among the no-
bility, clergy, and freeholders:—a felicity which
once occurred to myself, when the inhabitants of
Surrey were invited to assist the gentry in crying
down the Income Tax.

Thus, having no elective franchise, an English
farmer can scarcely be said to have a political
existence, and political *duties* he has none, except such, as under existing circumstances,
would inevitably consign him to the special
guardianship of the Secretary of State for the
home department.

In exchanging the condition of an English
farmer for that of an American proprietor,
I expect to suffer many inconveniences; but
I am willing to make a great sacrifice of
present ease, were it merely for the sake of
obtaining in the decline of life, an exemption
from that wearisome solicitude about pecuniary
affairs, from which, even the affluent find no

refuge in England ; and for my children, a career of enterprize, and wholesome family connections, in a society whose institutions are favourable to, virtue : and at last the consolation of leaving them efficient members of a flourishing, public-spirited, energetic community, where the insolence of wealth, and the servility of pauperism, between which, in England, there is scarcely an interval remaining, are alike unknown.

That institutions favourable to virtue, shall produce effects correspondent to their character upon the society blessed with them, is a conclusion so natural, that we should be inclined to suspect an error in our estimate of the institutions themselves, if we found a vicious people under a good government.

It is possible, however, that political virtue may exist in considerable purity, where the moral sense has been depraved by pre-existing habits, still more powerful in their influence on the general character than political principles ; and such an effect I anticipate from the present establishment of slavery in the southern States, and its former toleration in all.

But if we find these states rank higher in the scale of morals than the West India colonies, where slavery prevails, but where political virtue can scarcely have an existence, and especially if they have improved with the improvement of their government, these States will afford a confirmation of the rule, that political virtue is a moral good ; whilst a superiority in the morals of those states where slavery has been abolished —shows, that slavery is, in truth, the bane of society.

With these anticipations I prepare myself for an introduction into the State of Virginia, which takes so high a position in the political scale, though under the deteriorating influence of this calamity.

May 2. After a series of baffling winds and boisterous weather, we find ourselves on the Western, or *inside* of the Gulph Stream, and of course not far from our destination. Yesterday the temperature of the air was 65, and of the water 71. To-day the air remains at 65, but the water has fallen to 50. We have, therefore, crossed this warm ocean river, which flows from the Gulph of Mexico with a northerly and north-easterly course, until it meets the melting ice to the south of the great Bank of Newfoundland.

May 3. Last night we lay at anchor in Hampton Roads, and this morning I accompanied the captain in the pilot-boat to Norfolk, fourteen miles off, to make entry of the ship at the Custom House. This is a large town of

10,000 inhabitants ; the streets are in right lines, sufficiently spacious, with wide paved causeways before the houses, which are good-looking and cleanly. A large market-house in the centre of the principal street, with negroes selling for their masters, fine vegetables, and bad meat— the worst I ever saw, and dearer than the best in England. Veal, such as never was exposed in an English market, 10½d. per lb. ; lamb of similar quality and price. Most wretched horses waiting, without food or shelter, to drag home the carts which had brought in the provisions ; — but, worst of all, the multitudes of negroes, many of them miserable creatures, others cheerful enough ; but on the whole, this first glimpse of a slave population is extremely depressing : And is it, thought I, to be a member of such a society that I have quitted England !

Norfolk is fourteen miles from our anchorage off Cape Comfort. The pilot-boat took us thither in sixty-five minutes, and was about the same time in returning. After dinner, we proceeded about twenty miles up James River, towards City Point, which is our destination ; about one hundred from its mouth, and fifty below Richmond.

The river with its edging of pines and cedars, of various tints, which seem to grow out of the water, so low is the country,—is grand and beautiful, beyond all that I had conceived of American rivers. Although perfectly flat, the indentures of its course relieve the scenery from the dullness, that a continuance of pines on a level surface would otherwise occasion.

May 4. Forty-three miles up Cape Henry, where we passed the night, the river is still fourteen miles in breadth. This day we proceeded fifty-three miles.

The improving character of the country, and the indescribable beauty of the river, render our voyage extremely pleasant. I was employed with a telescope incessantly, exploring every cultivated spot, and every habitation;—so interesting is all that we behold on our first introduction to a foreign land. Plantations are more numerous, and the buildings much more respectable as we advance. The banks of the river are no longer a mere fringe of pines, but soil of a good quality, rising in some places many feet above the surface, and covered with timber of various sorts, locust, mulberry, walnut, sycamore, &c. A fondness for planting discovers itself even in this wilderness of trees. The Lombardy poplar, is a favourite accompaniment to the best mansions, rising in gloomy columns to a great height above the surrounding forest.

We passed Little Guinea, a tract given by

a planter to his negroes whom he liberated. We saw many of their cabins, and small inclosures, which appeared to be but indifferently cultivated. This gentleman's proceeding was not well relished by his neighbours ; and the negroes have a bad character for thieving,— deservedly I dare say, for slavery is a school of depravity, and their equivocal or degraded station among whites, is unfavourable to their moral improvement.

There are along the river the ruins of many houses, which I was told had been accidentally burnt by the negroes, whose carelessness is productive of infinite mischief.

May 6.   Harrison's Bar.—This is a shoal of mud, which greatly impedes the navigation, and in which we must be contented to lie until the next tide, and we may easily content ourselves, as it is a bend of the river, which is surrounded by all that is beautiful in woodland scenery, in the gayest dress of spring.   We are fixed about the middle of the stream, which is four miles wide.   Several rich plantations and substantial dwellings are in view.   We made a morning call on Mr.——and sat an hour with the ladies.   The well cultivated fields, and the goodness and comfort of the entire establishment gave us all great pleasure, and reminding us of home, seemed to assure us of homes in America.

As a security from fire, or to favour escape from it, a ladder is fixed on the roof, reaching from a garret window to the ridge, and down the other side :—It is an expedient in many houses, and denotes extraordinary fear, or extraordinary danger. I was informed, that the carelessness of the negroes rendered such precautions necessary.

May 7. Vessels at City Point, are under the superintendance of the Custom House at Petersburg, about 15 miles distant. It was necessary for me to attest to the contents of my baggage, and for the captain to enter his cargo: so we hired a gig, of which I took the command and proceeded to Petersburg. As my baggage was bulky enough to contain merchandize to a large amount, which would have been liable to a duty of nearly 30 per cent., I have to commend the liberality of the officers who suffered it to pass on my affidavit, without opening.

Petersburg is growing into a place of importance, being the emporium of export and import to a large district. Tobacco is the staple produce; and every article of British or German manufacture, the return.

It is not quite two years since half the town was destroyed by a fire, occasioned by some negroes playing at cards in a stable, and it is already nearly rebuilt in the most substantial manner. Two hundred capital brick houses were built last year. This vigorous revival under a calamity so general is a strong proof of general prosperity.

It was the time of the races at Petersburg, which gave me the opportunity of seeing a large assemblage of planters, and of being introduced to a considerable number of well-informed persons of that class.

A Virginian tavern resembles a French one with its table d'hôte, (though not in the excellence of its cookery) but somewhat exceeds it in filth, as it does an English one in charges. The daily number of guests at the ordinary in this tavern (and there are several large taverns in Petersburg) is fifty, consisting of travellers, store-keepers, lawyers, and doctors.

A Virginian planter is a republican in politics, and exhibits the high-spirited independence of that character : but he is a slave-master, irascible, and too often lax in morals, A dirk is said to be a common appendage to the dress of a planter in this part of Virginia.

I never saw in England an assemblage of countrymen who would *average* so well as to dress and manners: none of them reached any thing like style ; and very few descended to the shabby.

As it rained heavily, every body was confined

the whole day to the tavern, after the race, which took place in the forenoon. The conversation which this afforded me an opportunity of hearing, gave me a high opinion of the intellectual cultivation of these Virginian farmers.

Negro slavery was the prevailing topic—the beginning, the middle and the end—an evil uppermost in every man's thoughts ; which all deplored, many were anxious to fly, but for which no man can devise a remedy. One gentleman, in a poor state of health, dared not encounter the rain, but was wretched at the thought of his family being for one night without his protection —from his own slaves ! He was suffering under the effects of a poisonous potion, administered by a negro, who was his personal servant, to whom he had given indulgences and privileges unknown to the most favoured valet of an English gentleman. This happened in consequence of some slight unintentional affront on the part of the indulgent master. It is stated as a melancholy fact, that severe masters seldom suffer from their slaves' resentment.

This day the captain paid off the crew, who, almost to a man, immediately assembled round the grog store of the village, and having escaped from the restraints of discipline, and taken in a copious supply of whiskey, they engaged in a general fight, and shewed themselves

to be little better than a ferocious banditti, with
whom we had been so long cooped up, within
the narrow limits of the vessel.

May 9. The steam-boat which plies between
Norfolk and Richmond received us about nine
o'clock in the morning ; and, with some feeling
of regret we took a final leave of the good ship
America, but not of our captain, who was to re-
join us at Richmond.

The steam-boat is a floating hotel fitted up with
much taste and neatness, with accommodations
for both board and lodging. The ladies have
their separate apartment and a female to attend
them. Here we found ourselves at once in the
society of about thirty persons, who appeared to
be as polite, well dressed, and well instructed
as if they had been repairing to the capital of
Great Britain, instead of the capital of Virginia.
We had a delightful passage, and reached
Richmond about seven o'clock in the evening.

May 10. After delivering sundry letters of
introduction, we were anxious to secure a retreat from the crowded tavern which received
us from the steam-boat last evening. The elegant and cool abodes of the agreeable people to
whom we had presented our recommendatory
letters, formed such a contrast with the heat
and bustle of an inn, that we were determined,
at all events, to make our escape before the

approach of another night. After searching the
town through and through, we made our retreat
most gladly into two rooms in a lodging house,
where we were the more comfortable, from
having learnt on board ship, to find many conveniences in a narrow space.

Richmond contains 13,000 inhabitants, nearly
half of which are negroes. The hill, on which
stands the Capitol, a building of commanding
aspect, is inhabited by the more opulent merchants, and professional men, who have their
offices in the lower town. Their houses are
handsome, and elegantly furnished; and their
establishments and style of living display much
of the refinement of polished society. The
town is generally well built, and increasing
rapidly, whilst but little provision seems to be
made in the country round for the accommodation
of its inhabitants. The market is badly supplied:
the common necessaries of life are excessively
dear, and, excepting the article of bread, of bad
quality. Eggs are $2\frac{1}{2}d$. each; butter, 3s. 6d.
per lb.; meat, of the worst description, 1s. per
lb.; milk $4\frac{1}{2}d$, a pint: hay is two dollars (9s.)
per 100 lb. It is worse supplied and at a dearer
rate than any other place of equal size in the
United States, or perhaps in the world.

The town is forced up by the stimulus of commerce, whilst the surrounding country is groaning

under the torpid influence of slavery : the culti-
vators are said to be jealous of its rising prosperity, instead of availing themselves, as they
might, of the advantages it would afford as a
market for their produce.

House rent is high beyond example ; that
in which we have apartments, though in a back
street, and not very large or well finished, lets
at 1400 dollars, or 300 guineas a-year ; a
warehouse, or store, is commonly £200 a-year.
In short, the demand for town accommodations
of every kind, arising from the accession of
strangers, greatly exceeds the supply, though
building is going on in every direction. Ground
sells currently on building speculations, at 10,000
dollars per acre, and in some of the streets near
the river, at 200 dollars per foot in front.

The enterprizing people are mostly strangers ;
Scotch, Irish, and especially New England
men, or Yankees, as they are called, who fill
every house as soon as it is finished.

About 25,000 hogsheads of tobacco and
200,000 barrels of flour have been the yearly
export of the country through the hands of the
merchants of Richmond ; and probably a great
part of the proceeds may have returned through
the same channel in articles of import. This,
added to the internal consumption of a large
town, and of the shipping employed in this

commerce, forms an aggregate of great importance. The falls of James River, extending for five miles above Richmond, afford admirable mill seats. There are several fine flour mills : some of them turn eight pair of stones, and can grind and dress 1000 barrels of flour per week. To grind 95 bushels of wheat per day is reckoned the work of a pair of stones. A canal is formed by lockage parallel with these rapids, by which produce is brought down in long barges, capable of containing twenty-five hogsheads of tobacco.

May 10. 1 saw two female slaves and their children sold by auction in the street,—an incident of common occurrence here, though horrifying to myself and many other strangers. I could hardly bear to see them handled and examined like cattle ; and when I heard their sobs, and saw the big tears roll down their cheeks at the thought of being separated, I could not refrain from weeping with them. In selling these unhappy beings little regard is had to the parting of the nearest relations. Virginia prides itself on the comparative mildness of its treatment of the slaves ; and in fact they increase in numbers, many being annually supplied from this state to those farther south, where the treatment is said to be much more severe. There are regular dealers, who buy them up and drive them in gangs, chained together, to a southern market. I am informed that few weeks pass without some of them being marched through this place. A traveller told me that he saw, two weeks ago, one hundred and twenty sold by auction, in the streets of Richmond ; and that they filled the air with their lamentations.

It has also been confidently alledged that the condition of slaves in Virginia, under the mild treatment they are said to experience, is preferable to that of our English labourers. I know and lament the degraded state of dependent poverty, to which the latter have been gradually reduced, by the operation of laws originally designed for their comfort and protection. I know also, that many slaves pass their lives in comparative ease, and seem to be unconscious of their bonds, and that the *most wretched* of our paupers might envy the allotment of the *happy* negro : this is not, however, instituting a fair comparison, to bring the opposite extremes of the two classes into competition. Let us take a view of some particulars which operate generally.

In England, exertion is not the result of personal fear : in Virginia, it is the prevailing stimulus.

The slave is punished for mere *indolence,* at the discretion of an *overseer* :—The peasant is only punished by the law when guilty of a crime.

In England, the labourer and his employer are equal in the eye of the law. Here, the law affords the slave no protection, unless a white man gives testimony in his favour.

Here, any white man may insult a black with impunity ; whilst the English peasant, should he receive a blow from his employer, might and would return it with interest, and afterwards have his remedy at law for the aggression.

The testimony of a peasant weighs as much as that of a lord in a court of justice ; but the testimony of a slave is never admitted at all, in a case where a white man is opposed to him.

A few weeks ago, in the streets of Richmond, a friend of mine saw a white boy wantonly throw quick-lime in the face of a negro-man. The man shook the lime from his jacket, and some of it accidentally reached the eyes of the young brute. This casual retaliation excited the resentment of the brother of the boy, who complained to the slave's owner, and actually had him punished with thirty lashes. This would not have happened to an English peasant.

I must, however, do this justice to the slave-master of Virginia : it was not from him that I ever heard a defence of slavery ; some extenuation on the score of expediency, or necessity, is the utmost range now taken by that description tion of reasoners, who, in former times, would have attempted to support the principle as well as the practice.

Perhaps it is in its depraving influence on the moral sense of both slave and master, that slavery is most deplorable. Brutal cruelty, we may hope, is a rare and transient mischief; but the degradation of soul is universal, and, as it should seem, from the general character of free negroes, indelible.

All America is now suffering in morals through the baneful influence of negro slavery, partially tolerated, corrupting justice at the very source.

May 13. Here is a grand stir about a monument to the memory of General Washington, and about transferring his remains from their own appropriate abode to the city of Richmond; as though Washington could be forgotten whilst America retains her independence! Let republicans leave bones, and relics, and costly monuments to monks and kings: free America is the mausoleum of its deliverers, who may say to posterity, " *Si quæris monumentum circumspice.*"

It would be well, however for the patriots of Richmond to repair the mutilated bust of La Fayette in their Capitol, which now stands an object of horror and derision :—La Fayette, the friend of their hero, and his faithful, disinterested, and zealous associate.

There is a common feeling, a political sympathy between the wealthy federalists of the American *cities*, and the loyal anti-reformists of Great Britain. Federalism seems to favour a sort of whiggish aristocracy; but the spirit of the people at large, and of the ruling part in the government, is of a different complexion.

The society here is good, but not remarkable for intellectual activity ; yet, if literary pursuits are in no great request with the citizens of Richmond, they are eminent in urbanity and real politeness.

May 15. Accompanied Dr. A. with a party of his friends to the Chickahoming river, to view an improvement which he has conducted on a new principle. He has cleared one hundred and forty acres of marshy land, by simply girdling the trees, hoeing the surface, and sowing herb-grass ; (an agrostis, I fancy, but could not find it in bloom :) this is the second year, and he expects to mow two tons of hay per acre, which will be worth at Richmond, five or six miles off, eighteen pounds sterling.

This extraordinary profit is owing to the strange state of things at this place, where the supply of the commonest articles is inadequate to the demand ; but I believe it to be the right mode of management of land favourable for grass, where grain is low and labour high.

May 16. Visited Mr. W's. farm, about twelve miles up the river, above Richmond : on it are three hundred acres of wheat, as clean and good as I ever saw on one farm in any country, and a large breadth of good clover ; Indian corn, to a great extent very effectually cultivated with the horse and hand hoe ; and, on the whole, with the exception of live stock, which is neglected, I saw as good husbandry as would be expected in some well-managed districts in Great Britain.

A flat of rich alluvial soil, about a mile in breadth, accompanying the river, is the only part of this country that appears to be worth cultivating : the rest is for the most part a pine forest, as poor nearly as our heaths, extending from the sea coast to the high country, which skirts the Alleghany mountains. The soil of these high lands is strong and fruitful, forming the most agreeable portion of the state.

Something like the above character, I have been informed, is applicable to the Atlantic country generally.

May 19. In two hacks, which are light coaches with two horses, and a Jersey waggon and one horse for the baggage, we have had a

pleasant journey of two days to this place: the
distance sixty-nine miles.

Expence of Carriages .... 70 Dollars
————— on the Road 33
———
103

This, for nine persons, amounts to almost
fifty-two shillings sterling each ; dear, but very
agreeable travelling.

The country, from Richmond to Fredericksburg is a barren sandy level, relieved occasionally by a stripe of better soil, on the banks of a
rivulet, and near the latter place by a little un-
dulation of surface, and a soil containing reddish
loam.

The road would be good, during great part
of the year, if a small degree of attention was
directed to particular spots, trifling in extent,
but very dangerous.

Neglect of the public convenience and safety,
where little more is wanting than attention, at-
taches blame and disgrace somewhere. A few
dollars properly applied to a fault or two on the
road to City Point from Petersburg, would
render it safe, and even delightful :—the same
of the road from Richmond to Fredericksburg.
Works of great extent and cost may not suit
the state of this country, where the scope for
improvement is so vast in proportion to the

means; but the neglect of these petty local improvements, so essential to the comfort and safety of travellers, appears unpardonable!

On taking leave of Virginia, I must observe, that I found more misery in the condition of the negroes, and a much higher tone of moral feeling in their owners than I had anticipated; and I depart confirmed in my detestation of slavery, in principle and practice; but with esteem for the general character of the Virginians.

From Fredericksburg we took the stage to the River Potowmack, where we were received by the Washington steam-boat. This country is hilly and extremely pleasant, the soil not naturally rich, and seems to be exhausted by severe cropping. Our ride afforded new perils, which might be prevented at a small expence, and which now serves to evince the excellence of the drivers and horses, and the wonderful strength of their slight-looking vehicles.

The Potowmack, upwards, from our entering the steam-boat, flows through a bold country, and its banks are adorned with houses in fine situations, among which stands conspicuous Mount Vernon, the residence of the illustrious Washington.

The Federal City contains, including George Town, which is only separated from it by a

creek, about 20,000 inhabitants, scattered over
a vast space, like a number of petty hamlets in
a populous country. The intended streets,
radiating from the capital in right lines, are, for
the most part, only distinguishable from the
rugged waste by a slight trace, like that of a
newly-formed road, or in some instances by
rows of Lombardy poplars, affording neither
ornament nor shade, but evincing the exotic
taste of the designer.

The Capitol and the President's house are
under repair from the damage sustained in the
war. Ninety marble capitals have been imported
at vast cost from Italy to crown the columns of
the Capitol, and shew how *un*-American is the
whole plan. There is nothing in America to
which I can liken this affectation of splendor,
except the painted face and gaudy head-dress
of a half-naked Indian.

This embryo metropolis, with its foreign
decorations, should have set a better example to
the young republic, by surrounding itself first
with good roads and substantial bridges, in lieu
of those inconvenient wooden structures and
dangerous roads, over which the legislators
must now pass to their duty. I think too, that
good taste would have preferred native decora-
tion for the seat of the legislature.

From Washington to Fredericktown, in Maryland (45 miles) the country is poor, rugged, and badly cultivated, until we approach the latter, where limestone first appears, and with it an obvious improvement in soil and culture. Here begins a most beautiful district, extending through Hagar's Town to the Blue Ridge. This is rather a hilly than a mountainous country, though approaching the character of mountain in its formation, which is mica, and clay-slate, alternating with limestone.

McConnell's Town, May 23. The road we have been travelling terminates at this place, where it strikes the great turnpike from Philadelphia to Pittsburg ; and, with the road, ends the line of stages, by which we have been travelling ; a circumstance of which we knew nothing, until our arrival here, having entered ourselves passengers at George Town for Pittsburg, by the Pittsburg stage, as it professed to be.

So here we are, nine in number, one hundred and thirty miles of mountain country between us and Pittsburg. We learn that the stages which pass daily from Philadelphia and Baltimore are generally full, and that there are now many persons at Baltimore waiting for places. No vehicles of any kind are to be hired, and here we must either stay or *walk* off : the latter we prefer ; and separating each our bundle,

from the little that we have of travelling stores,
we are about to undertake our mountain pilgrimage ; accepting the alternative most cheerfully, after the dreadful shaking of the last
hundred miles by stage.

This is called the Alleghany Ridge, which
is loftier than the Blue Ridge, is apparently
newer in formation : its composition is chiefly
sand-stone, clay-slate, and limestone-slate ; the
latter with lamina of petrosilex parallel to the
limestone.

Maryland and Pennsylvania abound with
horses of the good old English breed ; with
great bone, of beautiful form, and denoting a
strain of high blood. The old English hunter
raised to a stout coach-horse, but comprising
all degrees of strength and size down to hackneys of fourteen hands. None of those wretched
dog-horses, which disgrace Virginia, are to be
seen here.

We have now fairly turned our backs on the
old world, and find ourselves in the very stream
of emigration. Old America seems to be breaking up, and moving westward. We are seldom out of sight, as we travel on this grand
track, towards the Ohio, of family groups,
behind and before us, some with a view to a
particular spot, close to a brother perhaps, or a
friend, who has gone before, and reported well

of the country. Many like ourselves, when they arrive in the wilderness, will find no lodge prepared for them.

A small waggon (so light that you may almost carry it, yet strong enough to bear a good load of bedding, utensils and provisions, and a swarm of young citizens,—and to sustain marvellous shocks in its passage over these rocky heights) with two small horses; sometimes a cow or two, comprises their all; excepting a little store of hard-earned cash for the land office of the district; where they may obtain a title for as many acres as they possess half-dollars, being one fourth of the purchase money. The waggon has a tilt, or cover, made of a sheet, or perhaps a blanket. The family are seen before, behind, or within the vehicle, according to the road or weather, or perhaps the spirits of the party.

The New Englanders, they say, may be known by the cheerful air of the women advancing in front of the vehicle; the Jersey people by their being fixed steadily within it; whilst the Pennsylvanians creep lingering behind, as though regretting the homes they have left. A cart and single horse frequently afford the means of transfer, sometimes a horse and pack-saddle. Often the back of the poor pilgrim bears all his effects, and his wife follows, naked-footed, bending under the hopes of the family.

The mountain tract we have passed is exceedingly romantic, as well as fertile, and is generally cultivated in a good style, excepting the rudest parts. It would be a delightful country to inhabit, but for the rigour of the winter. The temperature of the spring is 50 : at Richmond it was 57.

A blacksmith here earns 20 dollars per month, and board ; and he lives in a cabin of one room, for which, with a garden, he pays 20 dollars a year. Fire-wood is two dollars per cord :—the price is merely the labour, as is, in fact, a great part of what you pay for every thing. Thus, nothing but land is cheap in this country, excepting British goods, and they are not cheap to the consumer, because the store-keeper sells his own labour at a dear rate. Land will long be at a low price, but as produce hardly keeps pace with the population, the latter is proportionably dear. Therefore agriculture is and will be a safe and profitable occupation. As to manufactures, they will rise as they are wanted, and if they rise spontaneously, they will flourish without extraneous aid.

There cannot, as yet, be much capital to spare, for any kind of manufacture ; and it appears to be bad policy to *encourage*, as it is called, particular branches; because the direct consequence of this partial favour is, the diverting a portion of the scanty capital from those which need no encouragement, and to employ it where the profits are precarious. By such officious interference, a real good in possession, is sacrificed for a doubtful speculation,—substance for shadow.

May 26. We have completed our third day's march to general satisfaction. We proceed nearly as fast as our fellow-travellers in carriages, and much more pleasantly, so that we have almost forgotten our indignation against the pitiful and fraudulent stage-master of George Town; so apt are we to measure the conduct of other people, by the standard of our convenience, rather than its own merit.

This is a land of plenty, and we are proceeding to a land of *abundance*, as is proved by the noble droves of oxen we meet, on their way from the western country to the city of Philadelphia. They are kindly, well-formed, and well-fed animals, averaging about six cwt.

A flock of sheep, properly speaking, has not met my eyes in America; nor a tract of good sheep pasture. Twenty or thirty half-starved creatures are seen now and then straggling about in much wretchedness. These supply a little wool for domestic use. Cattle are good and plentiful, and horses excellent.

May 27. Stotler's Inn, summit of the Alleghany Ridge. Temperature of springs 47, Farenheit :—air at noon 73.

Cherries in blossom:

Kalmia latifolia in bud :

Laurustinus coming into bloom:

Trees in general bursting their buds, or shewing the tender leaf.

At City Point, below Richmond, Virginia, kalmia latifolia was in full bloom on the 5th of May; and early cherries were ripe at Richmond on May the tenth.

The Alleghany mountains are chiefly schistose. Clay-slate predominates, then mica-slate, limestone-slate, and sand-stone-slate. The schistose character is interrupted in some places, by tracts of sand-stone in large blocks ; the sand-stone appears to be a secondary formation from the disintegration of mica-slate.

This entire mountainous range is distinguished from all others that I have seen, by its being almost entirely covered by wood. The slaty formation affords great facility to the growth of trees, and may account for this peculiarity.

May 28. The condition of the people of America is so different from aught that we in Europe have an opportunity of observing, that it would be difficult to convey an adequate notion of their character.

They are great travellers; and in general, better acquainted with the vast expanse of country, spreading over their eighteen states, (of which Virginia alone nearly equals Great Britain in extent,) than the English with their little island.

They are also a migrating people; and even when in prosperous circumstances, can contemplate a change of situation, which under our old establishments and fixed habits, none, but the most enterprising, would venture upon, when urged by adversity.

To give an idea of the internal movements of this vast hive, about 12,000 waggons passed between Baltimore and Philadelphia, in the last year, with from four to six horses, carrying from thirty-five to forty cwt. The cost of carriage is about seven dollars per cwt., from Philadelphia to Pittsburg, and the money paid for the conveyance of goods on this road, exceeds £300,000 sterling. Add to these the numerous stages loaded to the utmost, and the innumerable travellers, on horseback, on foot, and in light waggons, and you have before you a scene of bustle and business, extending over a space of three hundred miles, which is truly wonderful.

When, on our voyage, we approached within twenty leagues of the American coast, we were cheered by the sight of ships in every direction.

Up James River, vessels of all sorts and sizes, from five hundred tons downwards, continually passing; and steam-boats crowded with passengers. The same on the Potowmack: and in the winter, when the navigation is interrupted by frost, stages, twelve or fourteen in file, are seen posting along, to supply the want of that luxurious accommodation.

But what is most at variance with English notions of the American people, is the urbanity and civilization that prevail in situations remote from large cities. In our journey from Norfolk, on the coast of Virginia, to this place, in the heart of the Alleghany mountains, we have not for a moment lost sight of the manners of polished life. Refinement is unquestionably far more rare, than in our mature and highly cultivated state of society; but so is extreme vulgarity. In every department of common life, we here see employed persons superior in habits and education to the same class in England.

We received the first impression of this superiority from the character of the pilot, whom we welcomed on board off Cape Henry: he was a well-informed and agreeable man; as we should have said, much above his station; but in this we should have erred, for we found his comrades of a similar description. Next occurred the custom-house officer, who was a gentlemanly youth, without a shade of the disagreeable character which prevails among his European brethren. He staid with us several days, and was succeeded by a second of the same respectable stamp. These officers of revenue are better paid here than with us ; and are considered as respectable persons, employed in an honourable service, which they have no temptation to abuse. They receive about £250 sterling per annum ; and one, with a competent salary, performs, with fidelity, the part of three in England, who are employed as checks upon each other.

The taverns in the great towns east of the mountains which lay in our route, afford nothing in the least corresponding with our habits and notions of convenient accommodation : the only similarity is in the expence.

At these places all is performed on the gregarious plan : every thing is public by day and by night ;—for even night in an American inn affords no privacy. Whatever may be the number of guests, they must receive their entertainment *en masse*, and they must sleep *en masse*. Three times a-day the great bell rings, and a hundred persons collect from all quarters to eat a hurried meal, composed of almost as many dishes. At breakfast you have fish, flesh, and fowl, bread of every shape and kind, butter,

eggs, coffee, tea—every thing, and more than
you can think of. Dinner is much like the breakfast, omitting the tea and coffee; and supper is
the breakfast repeated. Soon after this meal,
you assemble once more, in rooms crowded with
beds, something like the wards of an hospital ;
where, after undressing in public, you are fortu-
nate if you escape a partner in your bed, in addition to the myriads of bugs, which you need
not hope to escape.

But the horrors of the kitchen, from whence
issue these shoals of dishes, how shall I describe,
though I have witnessed them.—It is a dark and
sooty hole, where the idea of cleanliness never
entered, swarming with negroes of all sexes and
ages, who seem as though they were bred there :
without floor, except the rude stones that support a raging fire of pine logs, extending across
the entire place ; which forbids your approach,
and which no being but a negro could face.

In your reception at a western Pennsylvania
tavern, there is something of hospitality combined with the mercantile feelings of your host.
He is generally a man of property, the head man
of the village, perhaps, with the title of Colonel ;
and feels that he confers, rather than receives, a
favour by the accommodation he affords ; and
rude as his establishment may be, he does not
perceive that you have a right to complain : what

he has you partake of, but he makes no apologies; and if you shew symptoms of dissatisfaction or disgust, you will fare the worse; whilst a disposition to be pleased and satisfied, will be met by a wish to make you so.

At the last stage, our party of eight weary pilgrims, dropping in as the evening closed, alarmed the landlady, who asked the ladies if we were not English, and said, she would rather not wait upon us,—we should be "difficult." However, she admitted us, and this morning, at parting she said she liked to wait on "such" English; and begged we would write to our friends and recommend her house. We were often told that we were not "difficult," like the English; and I am sure our entertainment was the better, because they found us easy to please.

May 29. Surrounded by all that is delightful, in the combination of the hilly woodlands and river scenery. At the junction of the Alleghany and Monongahala, forming by their union the Ohio, stands the " city of Pittsburg, the Birmingham of America." Here I expected to have been enveloped in clouds of smoke, issuing from a thousand furnaces, and stunned with the din of ten thousand hammers.

There is a figure of rhetoric adopted by the Americans, and much used in description;

It simply consists in the use of the present indicative, instead of the future subjunctive ; it is called *anticipation*. By its aid, what *may be* is contemplated, as though it were in actual existence. For want of being acquainted with the power and application of this figure, I confess I was much disappointed by Pittsburg. A century and a half ago, possibly, the state of Birmingham might have admitted of a comparison with Pittsburg. I conceive there are many, very many, single manufacturing establishments in Great Britan, of more present importance than the aggregate of those in this town : yet, taken as it is, without rhetorical description, it is truly a very interesting and important place. Steam engines of great efficiency are made here and applied to various purposes, and it contains sundry works:—iron-foundries, glass-houses, nail-cutting factories, &c. establishments, which are as likely to expand and multiply as the small acorn, planted in a good soil and duly protected, is to become the majestic oak, that " flings his giant arms amid the sky."

At present the manufacturers are under great difficulties, and many are on the eve of suspending their operations, owing to the influx of depreciated fabrics from Europe.

Pittsburg contains about 7000 inhabitants,

and is a place of great trade, as an entrepot for the merchandize and manufactures supplied by the eastern states, to the western. The inhabitants of Kentucky, Ohio, Indiana, and Illinois, are their customers, and continually increasing in their demands upon the merchants and the artisans of Pittsburg.

Journeymen in various branches—shoe-makers, tailors, &c., earn two dollars a-day. Many of them are improvident, and thus they remain journeymen for life. It is not, however, in absolute intemperance and profligacy, that they in general waste their surplus earnings; it is in excursions, or entertainments. Ten dollars spent at a ball is no rare result of the gallantry of a Pittsburg journeyman. Those who are steady and prudent advance rapidly. A shoe-maker of *my acquaintance,* that is to say, whom I employed, left Ireland, as poor as an Irish emigrant, four years ago,—staid one year in Philadelphia, then removed hither, and was employed by a master practitioner of the same calling, at twelve dollars per week.—He saved his money, married, paid his master, who retired on his fortune, three hundred dollars for his business, and is now in a fair way of retiring too: as he has a shop well stocked and a thriving trade, wholesale and retail, with vast profits.

The *low* Irish, as they are called even here, too often continue in their old habit of whiskey drinking; and, as in London, they fill the lowest departments of labour in the manufactures, or serve the bricklayers, &c. They are rude and abandoned, with ample means of comfort and independence; such is the effect of habitual degradation of character. The low Irish and the freed negro, stand at nearly the same degree on the moral scale, being depressed equally by early associations.

June 2. This evening I heard delightful music from a piano, made in this place, where a few years ago stood a fort, from which a white man durst not pass, without a military guard, on account of the Indians, who were then the hostile lords of this region. A few of that people still reside at no great distance, and have in a great measure, settled into the habits and manners of their new neighbours.

The simple produce of the soil, that is to say, grain, is cheap in America, but every other article of necessity and convenience is dear, in comparison. Travelling east of the mountains, indeed, to this place, is nearly as expensive as in England; quite disproportioned to the prices of provisions, and especially to the accommodations afforded; and the store keeper lays on a profit of 50 per cent. at least. This is a modification of the high rate of labour, arising from the cheapness of land, which affords the possession of independence and comfort at so easy a rate, that strong inducements of profit are required to detain men in the less agreeable occupations of a town, or under the perplexity and hazard of trade and manufactures.

In this manner it is, that emigrants are frequently exposed to difficulties before they have obtained a settlement. In this *cheap* country they expect to be able to live well upon a little money;—but their little money is spent before they begin to live as Americans.

Every service performed for one man by another, must be purchased at a high rate, much higher than in England : therefore as long as he is obliged to purchase more than he sells of this service, or labour, he is worse off than at home: but, the moment he begins to perform his part as an American, the balance will turn in his favour, and he will earn, in the plainest occupation, double his subsistence.

I have this moment before me, two Germans, widowers, with three young children each, whose case is very appropriate. They are mere labourers, and cannot speak English, and are therefore sufficiently destitute for the purpose of illustration. These two men were hired at

Philadelphia, by a respectable man (with whom I have contracted an acquaintance, through a common friend) and they are now together, master and men, on their way to his farm, near Croydon, in the state of Indiana. These men are engaged for two years, at eighty dollars per annum each, with all necessaries; viz. house, food, and cloathing, for themselves, and children. Thus, at the expiration of two years, they are possessed of thirty-six pounds sterling each, and their children growing up to be useful. With this they may pay the first deposit on farms of eighty or a hundred acres, build themselves cabins, and become freeholders and citizens. Mechanics, or artisans of the most simple kind, earn half as much more, and those of superior talents rise rapidly to wealth.

June 4. We have purchased horses for our party at fifty to sixty dollars, and are making preparations for proceeding through the state of Ohio, to Cincinnati.

It is more usual for a party, or even for individuals, who have no business on land, to pass down the Ohio. " Arks," of which hundreds are on the river, are procured of a size suitable for the number. They are long floating rooms, built on a flat bottom, with rough boards, and arranged within for sleeping and other accommodations- You hire boatmen and lay in provisions, and, on your arrival at the destined port, sell your vessel as well as you can, possibly at half cost. On the whole, when the navigation is good, this is pleasant and cheap travelling.

But we, putting health and information against ease and saving of expence, have unanimously given the preference to horse-back. After a fortnight's confinement under the heats of the day, and the dews of the night, the habit, we think, must be ill prepared for the effects of the new climate and country; but on our horses taking the journey easily, we shall become gradually seasoned to it, and fortified by the healthful exercise of both mind and body

Pittsburg is a cheap market for horses, generally rather more so than we found it: travellers from the east, often quit their horses here, and take the river for New Orleans, &c. ; and on the contrary, those from the west proceed eastward from this place, in stages. Thus, there are constantly a number of useful hackneys on sale. The mode of selling is by auction. The auctioneer rides the animal through the streets, proclaiming with a loud· voice, the biddings that are made as he passes along, and when they reach the desired point, or when nobody bids more, he closes the bargain.

A complete equipment is, in the first place, a pacing horse, a blanket under the saddle, another upon it, and a pair of saddle-bags with great coat and umbrella strapped behind.

Women of advanced age, often take long journeys in this manner, without inconvenience. Yesterday I heard a lady mentioned familiarly (with no mark of admiration) who is coming from Tenessee, twelve hundred miles, to Pittsburg with an infant; preferring horseback to boating up the river.

Tracing a line like that we have traced from Cape Henry to Pittsburg, does not give a qualification to describe a country; of this no man is more aware than myself. Yet the line truly marked, though no picture, may serve as a profile: and before I take my leave of Old America, as I am now about to do, and enter on the new regions of the west, I must strengthen it a little by a few general remarks.

It is an observation, familiar, I doubt not, to every attentive traveller, that the soils of countries lying at the feet of mountains, are formed of disintegrated materials, similar to those mountains, which may be traced pretty distinctly unless where the surface has been disturbed by rivers. The ridge, or rather series of ridges, which passes from north to south, covering a breadth of one hundred and fifty miles, more or less, of the space between the western rivers and the Atlantic, affords a grand illustration of this fact, on the portion which we traversed.

On ascending this elevated region from the east in Maryland, I saw, or supposed I saw, in the quartz-rock and the mica-slate, the remains of the great magazine, from whence had been derived the barren sands I had crossed, from the sea-coast to the commencement of the clayey district : and in the clay-slate of the mountains could be very distinctly traced, in their various gradations of colour, from faint yellow to deep red, the several tracts of clay soil, which intervene between the sandy level of the sea-coast, and the high country bordering on the mountain. Similar evidences occur in the clays and micaceous sands, to the west of the ridge, in our descent to Pittsburg, where commences a country which has long been under the sway of the rivers, and has received from them a new character.

June 5. Well mounted and well furnished with saddle-bags and blankets, we proceeded, nine in file, on our westward course to Washington. (Pennsylvania.)

Seventeen miles of our ride, to Gannonsburg, was chiefly over clayey hills wonderfully adapted to grass, but too stiff for profitable cultivation under the plough, in the present circumstances cf the country. The difficult roads will long render this beautiful district toilsome to its inhabitants, unless they wisely convert it into a grazing country.

From Cannonsburg to Washington, eight miles, is a very desirable tract, containing much excellent working, dry land, with fine meadows and streams. A valuable district,— full of coal and limestone.

June 7. Washington is a pretty thriving town, of 2500 inhabitants. It has a college with about a hundred students. From the dirty condition of the schools, and the appearance of loitering habits among the young men, I should suspect it to be a coarsely conducted institution. It must, however, be an unfavourable period to judge of its character, as it has just undergone a contest about the change of presidents, and the session is only commencing.

There is also a considerable concourse of free negroes, a class of inhabitants peculiarly ill suited to a seat of education.

Though this district is not without streams, they are irregular, frequently dry, and again overflowing. Recourse is therefore had to steam mills, of which here is a capital one at this place. A fine piece of machinery calculated, like the mills in general, in America, to perform the entire manufacture of flour, almost without the intervention of hands, between its reception in the form of wheat and its final deposit in barrels in the shape of flour. A portion of machinery is also applied to wool-carding, for the family manufactures of the neighbourhood.

As I am writing my journal, a respectable couple, well mounted and equipped, alight at our tavern : a farmer and his wife, from the neighbourhood of Cincinnati, going to visit their friends at New York and Philadelphia; a distance of seven hundred miles. As travellers in this sociable country are wont to do, we immediately communicate our several plans and become mutually interested. He tells me of a newly instituted society at Cincinnati, called the Emigrant Society, designed to obtain correct information, and communicate it to the poorer order of emigrants; and to protect them from imposition.

June 8. We were detained at Washington by the indisposition of one of our party, and to-day proceeded only twenty-two miles to Ninian Beall's Tavern. We now consider ourselves, though east of the Ohio, to have made an inroad on the western territory: a delightful region ;—healthy, fertile, romantic.

Our host has a small and simple establishment, which his civility renders truly comfortable. His little history may serve as an example of the natural growth of property in this young country.

He is about thirty; has a wife and three fine healthy children : his father is a farmer; that is to say, a proprietor, living five miles distant. From him he received five hundred dollars, and " began the world," in true style of American enterprize, by taking a cargo of flour to New Orleans, about two thousand miles, gaining a little more than his expences, and a stock of knowledge. Two years ago he had increased his property to nine hundred dollars; purchased this place ; a house, stable, &c. and two hundred and fifty acres of land (sixty-five of which are cleared and laid down to grass,) for three thousand five hundred dollars, of which he has already paid three thousand, and will pay the remaining five hundred next year. He is now building a good stable, and going to improve his house. His property is at present worth seven thousand dollars ; having gained, or rather grown, five thousand five hundred dollars in two years, with prospects of future accumulation to his utmost wishes. Thus it is that people here grow wealthy without extraordinary exertion, and without any anxiety.

June 10. Having crossed the Ohio, we have now fairly set our foot on the land of promise.

Since we left the mountains, which seem to be the first boundary line between Eastern and Western America, many tempting situations have presented themselves to our notice; but the long and severe winters, in this climate and elevation, form a weighty objection to settling in the western part of Pennsylvania. Slavery would exclude such settlers as ourselves from Kentucky; and the complication of claims has produced such confusion with regard to the titles of estates, as to form, independent of that insuperable bar, another strong objection to Kentucky, as the place of our retreat.

On entering the state of Ohio from Wheeling, we find a country beautiful and fertile, and affording to a plain industrious and thriving population, all that nature has decreed for the comfort of man. It contains rich land, good water, wholesome air ;—lime, coal, mills, navigation. It is also fully appropriated and thickly settled ; and land is worth from twenty to thirty dollars per acre. An advance of a thousand per cent., in about ten years! Small estates of about a hundred acres may be purchased, with their buildings and improvements, at about twenty-five dollars per acre. These " improvements," however, are of little value ; and looking forward for the interest of our families, and around us to make room for our English friends,

who may wish to settle in our neighbourhood,
we must pass on, until we reach the country
where good land is to be purchased, at the
government price of two dollars per acre; and
which, in return for a few temporary privations,
increases in value in a similar ratio.

A heavy fall of rain had rendered the roads
muddy, and the numerous crossings of the two
creeks between Beall's Tavern and Wheeling
rather troublesome. Wheeling is a considerable
but mean-looking town, of inns and stores, on
the banks of the Ohio. Here we baited our
horses, and took our noon's repast of bread and
milk; but had we crossed the river and made
our bait on the opposite side, we should have
escaped a drenching thunder-storm, which
caught us as we were ferrying over the second
channel. At this place the Ohio is divided into
two channels, of five hundred yards each, by an
island of three hundred acres.

We took shelter from the storm in a tavern
at the landing-place; and, having dried our
clothes by a good fire, we cheerfully resumed
our course, in hopes of a fine evening for our
ride of ten miles to St. Clairsville; but the
storm continuing, we rode nearly the whole of
the way under torrents. We had sundry foaming
creeks to ford, and sundry log-bridges to pass,
which are a sort of commutation of danger. We

had a very muddy road, over hills of clay, with thunder and rain during nearly the whole of this our first stage:—such thunder and such rain as we hear of, but seldom witness, in England:— and thus our party of nine cavaliers, five male and four female, made our gallant entree into the western territory. To see the cheerful confidence which our young people opposed to difficulties, so new to them, was, to me, a more agreeable sight at that time, than the fairest weather, the noblest bridges, and the best roads could have afforded. It was truly a gallant train, making their way in Indian file, through the tempest, across those rocky creeks, swelled with the fresh torrents that were pouring in on every side.

We were detained some days at St. Clairsville by the continued indisposition of our friend; a circumstance which rendered the town more interesting to us than many others of greater importance. It consists of about one hundred and fifty houses; stores, taverns, doctors' and lawyers' offices, with the dwellings of sundry artisans; as taylors, shoemakers, hatters, smiths, &c. Its chief street runs over one of the beautiful round fertile hills which form this country. The Court House, a handsome brick structure on the summit, has a cheerful and rather striking appearance. If the streets were paved it would

be a pretty town ; but it is just now mere mud
from the continued rains. An American town
is, however, on the whole, a disagreeable thing
to me ; and so indeed is an English one.

In the evening, a farmer (a man of fifteen
stone or upwards,) and his son, a lad of ten
years old, alighted at our tavern ; their horses
in high condition, looked as though they had
just come in from the neighbourhood ; but they
were, in fact, on their return from Philadelphia,
to their home, one hundred miles west of this
place. They had been eight days on their road
from Philadelphia, and had travelled at the rate
of forty-five miles per day. The gentleman and
lady with their son, whom we met at Washington on their way to New York, were proceeding
at the same rate : they had been six days from
Cincinnati, two hundred and seventy-two miles,
and their horses fresh as if they were on their
first stage. From what I have seen and heard,
I conclude that this rate of travelling is usual,
and that it is performed without difficulty ; and
I mention it in proof of the excellence of the
horses of this country. They are generally about
fifteen hands high, clean made and shapely,
often very handsome. They generally pace, or
" rack," as it is called, being taught that mode
of going in their breaking. Five miles an hour
is as much as they calculate on. They feed well ;

four or five gallons of oats per day, besides hay, with a good handful of salt, about twice a week. A poor horse is as rare here, as a fat one among the negroes of Virginia. A good six years old horse, sells for a hundred to a hundred and fifty dollars.

The rich clay of this country is very favourable to grass, and the pastures are extremely fine. When the timber is destroyed, a beautiful turf takes immediate possession of the surface; which is at the present time an uniform sheet, or rather fleece of white clover.

As I have passed along, the subject of emigration from Great Britain to the United States, has naturally been a primary object of my attention; an important subject, on which I am anxious to convey some information; and much more anxious that, as far as it shall go, this information shall produce no false impressions on the minds of my countrymen.

From what I have seen, and heard from others of America, east of the Alleghany mountains, I judge that artisans in general, will succeed in any part of it; and that labourers of every description will greatly improve their condition; in so much, that they will, if saving and industrious, soon lay by enough to tempt them to migrate still farther in quest of land, on which they may establish themselves as proprietors;

—That mercantile adventurers would be likely to succeed as well, but not better than in England; that clerks, lawyers, and doctors, would gain nothing by the exchange of countries : the same of master manufacturers in general.

The glimpse I have of these western regions gives me similar notions, but more decided, whether favourable or unfavourable, regarding the emigration of the above descriptions of persons.

As to the condition of farmers in the eastern states, I am not very particularly informed. (The southern or slave states, I consider as without the range of the present inquiry.) But from what I have learnt, I entertain great doubts of the exchange, on the whole, proving satisfactory to the British farmer; and I am clear that it would not be advisable for persons of any other description than farmers to remove from Great Britain to the eastern states, in order to practise agriculture.

As to the removal of a British farmer to this western country it would be premature to say much, expecting soon to be enabled to record my own proceedings : but I have no doubt of its being greatly to the advantage of an industrious working family to exchange a rented farm in England for a freehold, west of the Ohio. The working farmer, by the amount of capital required in England, as a renter, may *own* and cultivate a much better farm in this country.

Emigrants with small capitals are liable to great inconvenience, unless they have a particular situation provided for them by some precursor on whom they can depend. Money is powerful in this country in purchasing land, but weak in providing the means of living, except as to the bare necessaries of life. Thus the travelling expences of emigrants are heavy, in addition to the waste of time in long peregrinations.

June 11. In my stroll among the lovely inclosures of this neighbourhood, I called to enquire my way at a small farm-house, belonging to an old Hibernian, who was glad to invite me in for the sake of a little conversation. He had brought his wife with him from his native island, and two children. The wife was at a neighbour's on a " wool-picking frolic," which is a merry meeting of gossips at each other's houses, to pick the year's wool and prepare it for carding. The son and daughter were married, and well-settled; each having eight children. He came to this place fourteen years ago, before an axe had been lifted, except to make a blaze road, a track across the wilderness, marked by the hatchet on the trees, which passed over the spot where the town now stands. A free and independent American, and a warm politician, he now discusses the interests of the state as one concerned in its prosperity :—and so he is, for he owns one hundred and eighteen acres of excellent land, and has twenty descendants. He has also a right to scrutinize the acts of the government, for he has a share in its appointment, and pays eight dollars a year in taxes :— five to the general treasury, and three to his own country :—in all about four-pence per acre. He still inhabits a *cabin*, but it is not an *Irish* cabin.

As particular histories lead to correct general notions, I shall give another little tale of early difficulties, related to us by a cheerful intelligent farmer, from the neighbourhood of Chillicothe, who made one of our party at the inn this evening. Fourteen years ago, he also came into this new settlement, and " unloaded his family under a tree," on his present estate ; where he has now two hundred acres of excellent land, cleared and in good cultivation, capable of producing from eighty to one hundred bushels of Indian corn per acre.

The settlers in a country entirely new, are generally of the poorer class, and are exposed to difficulties, independent of unhealthy situations, which may account for the mortality that sometimes prevails among them. The land, when intended for sale, is laid out in the government surveys in quarter sections of 160 acres, being one fourth of a square mile. The whole is then offered to the public by auction, and that which remains unsold, which is generally a very large proportion, may be purchased at the land office of the district, at two dollars per acre, one fourth to be paid down, and the remaining three-fourths at several instalments, to be completed in five years.

The poor emigrant, having collected the eighty dollars, repairs to the land office, and enters his quarter section, then works his way without another "cent" in his pocket, to the solitary spot, which is to be his future abode, in a two horse waggon, containing his family, and his little all, consisting of a few blankets, a skillet, his rifle, and his axe. Suppose him arrived in the spring : after putting up a little log cabin, he proceeds to clear, with intense labour, a plot of ground for Indian corn, which is to be their next year's support ; but, for the present, being without means of obtaining a supply of flour, he depends on his gun for subsistence. In pursuit of the game, he is compelled, after his day's work, to wade through the evening dews, up to the waist, in long grass, or bushes, and returning, finds nothing to lie on but a bear's skin on the cold ground, exposed to every blast through the sides, and every shower through the open roof of his wretched dwelling, which he does not even attempt to close, till the approach of winter, and often not then. Under these distresses of extreme toil and exposure, debarred from every comfort, many valuable lives have sunk, which have been charged to the climate.

The individual whose case is included in this seeming digression, escaped the ague, but he lay three weeks delirious in a nervous fever, of which he yet feels the remains, owing, no doubt, to excessive fatigue. Casualties, doubly calamitous in their forlorn estate, would sometimes assail them. He, for instance, had the misfortune to break his leg at a time when his wife was confined by sickness, and for three days they were only supplied with water, by a child of two years old, having no means of communicating with their neighbours (neighbours of ten miles off perhaps) until the fourth day. He had to carry the little grain he could procure twelve miles to be ground, and remembers once seeing at the mill, a man who had brought his, sixty miles, and was compelled to wait three days for his turn.

Such are the difficulties which these pioneers have to encounter; but they diminish as settlements approach each other, and are only heard of by their successors. The number of emi-

grants who passed this way, was greater last
year than in any preceding ; and the present
spring they are still more numerous than the
last. Fourteen waggons yesterday, and thir-
teen to-day, have gone through this town.
Myriads take their course down the Ohio. The
waggons swarm with children. I heard to-day
of three together, which contain forty-two of
these young citizens. The wildest solitudes
are to the taste of some people. General Boon,
who was chiefly instrumental in the first
settlement of Kentucky, is of this turn. It
is said, that he is now, at the age of seventy,
pursuing the daily chase, two hundred miles to
the westward of the last abode of civilized man.
He had retired to a chosen spot, beyond the
Missouri, which, after him is named Boon's
Lick, out of the reach, as he flattered himself, of
intrusion; but white men, even there, incroached
upon him, and two years ago, he went back two
hundred miles further.

June 13. The soil does not improve as we
proceed westward, towards Zanesville. It is a
yellow clay, kindly for grass, but will be unpro-
fitable for tillage, when exhausted by repeated
cropping. In some places, the clay is over
limestone, and exhibits marks of great and
durable fertility.

Many of the dwellings on the road-side have

an air of neatness, and the roads themselves are better attended to than in Virginia, and the western parts of Pennsylvania; or even in the neighbourhood of the federal city, where they are so busily employed in ornamental architecture.

This morning we had the pleasure of meeting a group of nymphs with their attendant swains, ten in number, on horseback: (for no American walks who can obtain a horse, and there are few indeed, who cannot.) The young men were carrying umbrellas over the heads of their fair partners (*fair* by courtesy,) and as there was no shew of *Sundays' best* about them, we were the more pleased with their decent, respectable appearance.

We had also the pleasure of meeting a drove of very fat oxen on their way from the banks of the Miami to Philadelphia. They might on the average weigh six hundred pounds, cost about thirty dollars, and sell at Philadelphia at about fifty or fifty-five dollars per head.

June 14. Eighteen miles east of Zanesville, taking shelter from a thunder storm, we were joined by four industrious pedestrians, returning eastward from a tour of observation through this state, which is no unusual thing among labourers and artisans, who travel about, and stop occasionally to work at their callings, when their finances require a supply.

All agree in one sentiment, that there is no part of the union, in the new settlements or the old, where an industrious man need be at a loss for the comforts of a good livelihood. One of them, a hatter, resolves to remain in his old position, in Philadelphia. There are, in this western country, he says, more artisans than materials. Shoemakers are standing still for want of leather, and tanners for want of hides.

The land continues of the same character,—a weak yellow clay, under a thin covering of vegetable mould; profitable to cultivate, merely because it is new. Timber, chiefly oak. Little farms from eight to one hundred and sixty acres, with simple erections, a cabin and a stable, may be purchased at from five to twenty dollars per acre; the price being in proportion to the quantity of cleared land. This is a hilly, romantic country, and affords many very pleasant situations.

Sand-stone is frequent; limestone more rare; but clay-slate appears to be the common basis.

The inhabitants are friendly and homely, not to say coarse, but well-informed, surprisingly more so than the English peasantry. An agreeable, contented-looking cheerful man, who partook of our shelter, told us that he cultivated a little land to supply his family with eatables;

but mostly employed himself in making shingles, (wooden tiles) at which he earned a dollar and a half per day. He had been here eleven years. We must not judge of these respectable citizens from the tribe of loungers that haunt the taverns on the road side, to the annoyance of travellers·

Few's Tavern. We have penetrated about seventy miles into the state of Ohio. As we proceed, our astonishment increases at seeing so much done in so short a period. A gentleman who is now our companion of the way, travelled twelve years ago on this same track. It was then little more than an Indian path through the wilderness; though now it is a string of plantations, with but little intermission of uncleared tracts.

To-day we passed various groups of emigrants proceeding westward : one waggon, in particular, was the moving habitation of twenty souls.

June 15. Zanesville is a thriving town on the beautiful river Muskingum, which is at all times navigable downwards. The country around it is hilly, and very pleasant ; not rich, but dry, and tolerably fertile It abounds in coal and lime, and water-power for machinery : —a grand station for manufactures at a future period.

Somerset. A town of no great promise. Our landlord, a German, experienced the toils of the

earliest settlement, being the first who lifted the
axe in this neighbourhood. He went to the distance of fifty-four miles for flour, four times in
the first summer. He could get venison in plenty,
with his rifle ; but nothing else even for money.

The most perfect cordiality prevails between
the Americans of German and those of English
extraction, in every part of the United States, if
the assertions of all with whom I have conversed
on this interesting topic, are to be relied on.
National antipathies are the result of *bad political institutions*, and not of human nature.
Here, whatever their original, whether English,
Scotch, Irish, German, or French — all are
Americans : and of all the imputations on the
American character, jealousy of strangers is
surely the most absurd and groundless. The
Americans are sufficiently alive to their own interest, but they wish well to strangers ; and are
not always satisfied with wishing, if they can
promote their success by active services.

Land with some" improvements" (land cleared) is worth from twenty to thirty dollars per
acre.

Thus the poor man who entered his quarter
section of one hundred and sixty acres twelve
years ago, and had paid three hundred and
twenty dollars for it at the end of five, has supported his family, during this time, and now

finds himself worth from three to four thousand dollars, besides his moveable property. Such is the natural progress of an Ohio settler. ¹

In this proportion an increase of real wealth has taken place within the last twenty years, over a space greatly exceeding Great Britain in extent. Yet so *new* is the government of this new world in the art and mystery of finance, that the revenue derived from all this wealth, hardly exceeds forty shillings sterling, per square mile. The simple land tax is one dollar per hundred acres of first quality, and three fourths of a dollar per hundred for that of second quality.

June 16. Rushville. An American breakfast is in much the same style on the eastern coast of Virginia, and in the centre of the Ohio state : a multifarious collection of discordant dishes fatiguing to the mistress of the house in its preparation, and occasioning much unpleasant delay to the traveller.

A gentleman, myself, and three children sat down this morning to a repast, consisting of the following articles : coffee, rolls, biscuits, dry toast, waffles, (a soft hot cake, of German extraction, covered with butter) pickerell salted (a fish from Lake Huron) veal cutlets, broiled ham, gooseberry pie, stewed currants, preserved cranberries, butter and cheese : for all this, for myself, and three children, and four gallons of oats, and hay for four horses, we were charged six shillings and nine pence sterling.

Chillicothe. June 17. South West of Zanesville, instead of the steep hills of yellow clay, the country assumes a more gently undulating surface, but sufficiently varied for health and ornament, with an absorbent, gravelly, or sandy soil, of moderate fertility.

Lancaster is on the very edge of a marsh, or fen, a future meadow, which at present should seem to be a fruitful source of disease, though its bad effects on the inhabitants of that town are not by any means obvious.

These prairies which are constantly wet, are not understood to be so prejudicial to health, as the little marshy bottoms, on the borders of creeks, which are dried up, and again inundated by every succeeding freshet.

The three towns, Zanesville, Lancaster, and Chillicothe, were founded by a sagacious man of the name of Zane, one of the earliest of the settlers. They are admirably placed, geographically, but with little regard to the health of their future inhabitants. The local advantages of Zanesville might have been secured equally, had the scite of the town been on the higher rather than the lower bank of the Muskingum : and the Sciota might have afforded equal facilities to the commerce of the inhabitants of Chillicothe, had they viewed it flowing beneath them, from those lovely eminences which adorn its opposite banks. Chillicothe is surrounded by the most charming elevations, but is itself in a bottom. And Lancaster, as observed in passing it, is on the brink of an extensive marsh.

Gain! Gain! Gain! is the beginning, the middle and the end, the *alpha* and *omega* of the founders of American towns; who after all are bad calculators, when they omit the important element of salubrity in their choice of situations.

Seven miles N. W. of Chillicothe we enter on a tract of river bottom, the first-rate rich land, for which this state, and indeed the whole western country, is so justly famous. It is cool sand, sufficiently, but not too dry, easy of tillage, and, as far as is yet experienced, inexhaustibly fertile. It is agreeably varied in surface, rising into hills occasionally, and never flat. An alluvial sand, with calcareous and silicious gravel.

June 18. At Chillicothe is the office for the several transactions regarding the disposal of the public lands, of this district, which is a large tract, bounded on the west by the river Sciota. This business is conducted with great exactness, on a principle of checks, which are said to prevent the abuses formerly prevailing among the land-jobbers and surveyor. The following, if I am rightly informed, is an outline of the measures now adopted, in the sale of government lands.

The tract of country, which is to be disposed of, is surveyed, and laid out in sections of a mile square, containing six hundred and forty acres, and these are subdivided into quarters, and, in particular situations, half-quarters. The country is also laid out in counties of about twenty miles square, and townships of six miles square, in some instances, and in others eight. The townships are numbered in ranges, from north to south, and the ranges are numbered from west to east; and lastly, the sections in each township are marked numerically. All these lines are well defined in the woods, by marks on the trees. This done, at a period of which public notice is given, the lands in question are put up to auction, excepting the sixteenth section in every township, which is reserved for the support of schools, and the maintenance of the poor. There are also sundry reserves of entire townships, as funds for the support of seminaries on a more extensive scale; and sometimes for other purposes of general interest. No government lands are sold under two dollars per acre; and I believe they are put up at this price in quarter sections, at the auction, and if there be no bidding they pass on. The best lands and most favourable situations are sometimes run up to ten or twelve dollars, and in some late instances much higher. The lots which remain unsold are, from that time, open to the public, at the price of two dollars per acre; one-fourth to be paid down, and the remaining three-fourths to be paid by instalments in five years; at which time, if the payments are not completed, the lands revert to the state, and the prior advances are forfeited.

When a purchaser has made his election of one, or any number of vacant quarters, he repairs to the land office, pays eighty dollars, or as many times that sum as he purchases quarters, and receives a certificate, which is the basis of the complete title, which will be given him when he pays all; this he may do immediately, and receive eight per cent. interest for prompt payment. The sections thus sold are marked immediately on the general plan, which is always open at the land-office to public inspection, with the letters A. P. " advance paid." There is a receiver and a register at each land office, who are checks on each other, and are remunerated by a per centage on the receipts.

June 19. On my arrival at Chillicothe, I repaired to the land office, to inspect the map of the district, and found a large amount of uneutered lands, comprehending several entire townships of eight miles square, lying about twenty miles south of the town, and in several parts abutting on the Sciota. Though it appeared morally certain, that substantial objections have deterred purchasers from this extensive tract in a country so much settled : the distance being moderate, I determined to visit it, and am now with my son, resting at the cabin of a poor widow on the way. We have rode over twenty miles of very fertile country on the Sciota, and shall cross that river a few miles forward at Pike's Town; not far from which place is the land we are seeking.

I hear much of the agues and bilious fever, by which strangers are said to be generally naturalized or seasoned to these new countries; but the accounts are so contradictory, though equally authentic, that I conclude much of this disease is rather the effect of particular situations or circumstances, than of any general cause existing in the country or climate. There are a few facts on which all agree:—that the country becomes more healthy as it is more cleared and cultivated. That the neighbourhoods of rivers and creeks, subject to overflow, are the most unhealthy; and wet prairies the next: that dry soils and elevated situations are more healthy than those that are low or wet;

and that mill-ponds are frequently noxious to settlers in their vicinity. It is also universally allowed, that most of the diseases which attack new settlers may be justly attributed to their own poverty or imprudence. I have been conversing on this subject with our experienced old landlady, which led to these observations.

As we sat at breakfast we heard a report like the discharge of cannon. It was a sycamore, one of the largest and most ancient of the forest, which had just then arrived at its term, and fallen under the weight of age. It formed one of a venerable group, about a quarter of a mile from our cabin, and our hostess missed it instantly.

Trees are very interesting objects to the American traveller: they are always beautiful; and in the rich bottoms they sometimes exhibit a grand assemblage of gigantic beings which carry the imagination back to other times, before the foot of a white man had touched the American shore. Yesterday I measured a walnut tree almost seven feet in diameter, clean and straight as an arrow; and just by, were rotting, side by side, two sycamores of nearly equal dimensions! The sycamore grows, in bottoms liable to be overflowed, to an unwieldly bulk; but the white oak is the glory of the upland forest.

Trees, to the judicious and experienced observer, form an excellent criterion of the quality of soils, by their species as well as bulk; but in the American forests they have rarely an opportunity of swelling out to a large diameter, owing to their crowded growth. They are, for the same reason, very lofty, straight, and clear in their stems; sometimes eighty or ninety feet without a branch. I measured a white oak, by the road side, which, at four feet from the ground, was six feet in diameter, and seventy-five feet; it measured nine feet round, or three feet in diameter.

White oak is valuable for a great variety of uses; particularly where toughness is required; in proof of its possessing this quality in an extraordinary degree, it forms the material of an American waggoner's very flexible whip. A tapering piece of this wood is cleft in nine, from the small end to within a foot of the other end, which remains solid for the hand. The nine spleets are then twisted by threes, and the threes again twisted together: the whole is then sewed in a case of black leather, and a silken thong added, which completes the whip. This oak is also excellent for keels of ships, and shingles for covering houses, and a thousand other purposes; particularly for the wheels and poles of carriages; and enables the workman to unite strength and lightness, to a degree greatly excelling the justly admired carriages of England.

Near Pike Town is a small cultivated prairie, the first I have seen : it contains about two hundred acres, as I estimate it, of rich river bottom : it is divided by a road which runs through the middle, between two fences, and nearly the whole is covered by the finest Indian corn, neatly cultivated. The surrounding hills, crowned with their native woods, take their tone from the garden-like appearance of this inclosure, and the scene retains nothing of wildness, except in the untameable luxuriance of vegetation. Nothing I had before seen in America at all resembles this delightful spot ; but it has been unhealthy, and continues so, though in a less degree than at its first settlement, from its low situation near the Sciota.

The growth of timber round this prairie, and the under-growth of papaw, &c. is so thick, that not a blade of grass is to be found, and the surface is covered by persicaria. The cattle being left to provide for themselves, look miserable amid this exuberant fertility : but the settlers are mostly from Virginia ; where I saw so much wretchedness among the cattle that I suppose it is familiar to the inhabitants.

June 19. Pike Town. This town was laid out and received its name two years ago. It now contains a tavern, a store, and about twenty other dwellings. Being on the banks of the Sciota, half way between Chillicothe, and Portsmouth, which is at the junction of that river with the Ohio, it will probably grow into a place of importance.

The unentered land we came in quest of is, as I supposed, of inferior quality. That which abutts on the river, consists of sand-stone hills, without any portion of the rich alluvial bottom. The interior sections contain lands which might be useful as an appendage to better.

I found a cabin on a sandy brow, which had been inhabited eleven years, by the present family. It is in the neighbourhood of the small prairie, where there had been so much sickness; but they had always escaped, never experiencing the least inconvenience. An elevated situation on an absorbent soil, not buried too deeply in heavy timber, seems to afford the best security for health.

Though we find no land fit for our purpose, we are repaid by the pleasure of our ride through a fine portion of country; and especially by the information we pick up as we pass along. It is by multiplied observations that we must qualify ourselves to make a good final choice.

Greenfield, *June* 20. We are now again on

our way towards Cincinnati. In leaving Chillicothe, we pass through about seven miles of rich alluvial land, and then rise to fertile uplands. But as we proceed, the country becomes level, with a cold heavy soil, better adapted to grass than tillage. Much of this tract remains in an unimproved state.

Before we entered on this flat country, were some hills covered with the grandest white oak timber, I suppose, in America : (should I meet with any thing to compare with this hereafter, I shall not fail to note it.) There are thousands, I think, of these magnificent trees within view of the road for miles, measuring fourteen or fifteen feet in circumference : their straight stems rising without a branch, to the height of seventy or eighty feet, not tapering and slender, but surmounted by full luxuriant heads.

For the space of a mile in breadth, a hurricane, which traversed the entire western country in a north-east direction, about seven years ago, had opened itself a passage through this region of giants, and has left a scene of extraordinary desolation. We pass immediately on, after viewing those massive trunks, the emblems of strength and durability, to where they lie tumbled over each other like scattered stubble, some torn up by the roots, others broken off at different heights, or splintered only, and their tops bent over, and touching the ground :—such is the irresistable force of these impetuous airy torrents.

These hurricane tracts afford strong holds for game, and all animals of savage kind. There is a panther, the only one remaining, it is said, in this country, which makes this spot its haunt, and eludes the hunters.

I am told that the town of Greenfield has wholly escaped the sickness, so frequently attending new settlements. It stands on a hill, and on a dry soil.

June 21. Last night we lodged at Leesburg, a healthy, comfortable little colony of quakers, of four years standing. The soil is sandy, of middling quality, over limestone.

No instance of ague, or bilious fever, has yet occurred in this settlement. One of the friends informed me that he had carried his wife, who was an invalid, to the sulphur springs in Madison county, by the advice of a physician. The creek there frequently overflowed, and the country being flat, a considerable breadth was inundated. When that dried up, an offensive vapour rose, which might be perceived to a considerable distance. They both grew sick, and were in great danger, but he ordered his waggon, and had his wife and himself laid in it, and carried directly home to Leesburg :—they recovered immediately.

These are important cases, and I have no doubt of their authenticity. Greenfield never knew the sickness: Leesburg never knew it; but was even medicine for the ills occasioned by another situation, near an unwholesome over-flowing creek. Neither of these places stand high ; that is particularly so, but they are remote from floods ; and the soil lies over limestone, and is dry enough for the plough in half a day after heavy rain.

The first settlers, needy people, and ignorant of the dangers they were incurring, found good land along the course of the rivers ; and there they naturally fixed their cabins ; near enough to the stream to dip out of it with a bowl, provided they could escape the flood. The founders of towns seem to have generally chosen their situations on similar principles ; preferring convenience or profit to salubrity : and thus diseases, which, strictly speaking, are local, come to be considered universal and unavoidable.

June 22. As we approach the Little Miami river, the country becomes more broken, and much more fertile, and better settled. After crossing this rapid and clear stream we had a pleasant ride to Lebanon, which is not a mountain of cedars, but a valley, so beautiful and fertile, that it seemed on its first opening on our view, enriched as it was by the tints of evening, rather a region of fancy than a real backwood scene.

Lebanon is itself, one of those wonders which are the natural growth of these backwoods. In fourteen years, from two or three cabins of half-savage hunters, it has grown to be the residence of a thousand persons, with habits, and looks no way differing from their brethren of the east. Before we entered the town, we heard the supper bells of the taverns, and arrived just in time to take our seats at the table, among just such a set as I should have expected to meet at the ordinary in Richmond ;—travellers like ourselves, with a number of storekeepers; lawyers, and doctors;—men who board at the taverns, and make up a standing company for the daily public table.

This morning we made our escape from this busy scene, in defiance of the threatening rain. A crowded tavern in an American town, though managed as is that we have just quitted, with great attention and civility, is a place from which you are always willing to depart. After all, the wonder is, that so many comforts are provided for you, at so early a period.

Cincinnati, like most American towns, stands too low : it is built on the banks of the Ohio, and the lower part is not out of the reach of spring-floods.

As if " life was not more than meat, and the body than raiment," every consideration of health and enjoyment yields to views of mercantile convenience. Short-sighted and narrow economy; by which the lives of thousands are shortened, and the comfort of all sacrificed to mistaken notions of private interest !

Cincinnati is, however, a most thriving place, and backed as it is already by a great population and a most fruitful country, bids fair to be one of the first cities of the west. We are told, and we cannot doubt the fact, that the chief of what we see is the work of four years. The hundreds of commodious, well-finished brick houses, the spacious and busy markets, the substantial public buildings, the thousands of prosperous well-dressed, industrious inhabitants, the numerous waggons and drays, the gay carriages and elegant females ;—the shoals of craft on the river, the busy stir prevailing every where, houses building, boat building, paving and levelling streets ; the numbers of country people, constantly coming and going, with the spacious taverns, crowded with travellers from a distance.

All this is so much more than I could comprehend, from a description of a new town, just risen from the woods, that I despair of conveying an adequate idea of it to my English friends. It is enchantment, and Liberty is the fair enchantress.

I was assured by a respectable gentleman, one of the first settlers, and now a man of wealth and influence, that he remembers when there was only one poor cabin where this noble town now stands. The county of Hamilton is something under the regular dimensions of twenty miles square, and it already contains 30,000 inhabitants. Twenty years ago, the vast region comprising the states of Ohio and Indiana, and the territory of Illinois and Michigan, only counted 30,000 inhabitants; the number that are now living, and living happily, in the little county of Hamilton, in which stands Cincinnati.

Why do not the governments of Europe afford such an asylum, in their vast and gloomy forests, for their increasing myriads of paupers! This would be an object worthy a convention of sovereigns, if sovereigns were really the fathers of their people : but jealous as they are of emigration to America, this simple and sure mode of preventing it will never occur to them.

Land is rising rapidly in price, in all well-settled neighbourhoods. Fifty dollars per acre for improved land, is spoken of familiarly : I have been asked thirty for a large tract, without improvements, on the Great Miami, fifty miles from Cincinnati, and similar prices in other quarters. An estate of a thousand acres, partially cleared, is spoken of, on the road to Louisville, at twenty dollars. Many offers occur, all at a very great advance of price. It now becomes a question, whether to fix in this comparatively populous state of Ohio, or join the vast tide of emigration, that is flowing farther west, where we may obtain lands of equal value, at the government price of two dollars per acre, and enjoy the advantage of choice of situation.

Though I feel some temptation to linger here, where society is attaining a maturity truly astonishing, when we consider its early date, I cannot be satisfied without seeing that remoter country, before we fix in this; still enquiring and observing as we proceed. If we leave behind us eligible situations, it is like securing a retreat to which we may return with good prospects, if we think it advisable.

The probability is that, in those more remote regions, the accumulation of settlers will shortly render land as valuable as it is here at present; and in the interim, this accession of inhabitants will create a demand for the produce of the new country, equal to the supply. It is possible too, that we may find ourselves in as good society there as here. Well-educated persons are not rare amongst the emigrants who are moving farther west; for the spirit of emigration has reached a class somewhat higher in the scale of society than formerly. Some too may be aiming at the same point with ourselves; and others, if we prosper, will be likely to follow our example.

We are also less reluctant at extending our views westward, on considering that the time is fast approaching, when the grand intercourse with Europe, will not be, as at present, through eastern America, but through the great rivers which communicate by the Mississippi with the ocean, at New Orleans. In this view, we approximate to Europe, as we proceed to the west.

The upward navigation of these streams is already coming under the controul of steam, an invention which promises to be of incalculable importance to this new world.

Such is the reasoning which impels us still forward; and in a few days we propose setting out to explore the state of Indiana, and probably the Illinois. With so long a journey before us, we are not comfortable under the prospect of separation. Our plan had been to lodge our main party at Cincinnati, until we had fixed on our final abode: but this was before our prospects

had taken so wide a range. We now talk
of Vincennes, as we did before of this place,
and I trust we shall shortly be again under
weigh.

June 27. Cincinnati.—All is alive here as
soon as the day breaks. The stores are open,
the markets thronged, and business is in full
career by five o'clock in the morning ; and nine
o'clock is the common hour for retiring to rest.

As yet I have felt nothing oppressive in the
heat of this climate. Melting, oppressive, sultry
nights, succeeding broiling days, and forbidding
rest, which are said to wear out the frames of
the languid inhabitants of the eastern cities, are
unknown here. A cool breeze always renders
the night refreshing, and generally moderates
the heat of the day.

June 28. The numerous creeks in this country,
which are apt to be swelled suddenly by heavy
rains, render travelling perplexing, and even
perilous to strangers, in a showery season like
the present. On my way this morning from an
excursion of about fifteen miles, to view an estate,
a man who was mowing at some distance from
the road, hailed me with the common, but to us
quaint appellation of " stranger :"—I stopped
to learn his wishes. " Are you going to ride the
creek?" " I know of no creek," said I ; " but
I am going to Cincinnati."—" I guess it will

swim your horse." "How must I avoid it?"
" Turn to your left, and go up to the mill, and
you will find a bridge." Now if this kind man
had rested on his scythe, and detained the
" stranger" a few minutes, to learn his country,
his name, and the object of his journey, as he
probably would, had he been nearer to the road,
he would but have evinced another trait of the
friendly character of these good Americans.

In this land of plenty, young people first
marry, and then look out for the means of a
livelihood, without fear or cause for it. The
ceremony of marriage is performed in a simple
family way, in my opinion more delicate, and
corresponding to the nature of the contract, than
the glaring publicity adopted by some, or the
secrecy, not so respectable, affected by others.

The near relations assemble at the house of
the bride's parents. The minister or magis-
trate is in attendance, and when the candidates
make their appearance, he asks them severally
the usual questions, and having called on the
company to declare if there be any objections,
he confirms the union by a short religious for-
mula ;—the bridegroom salutes the bride, and
the ceremony is over. Tea and refreshments
follow. Next day the bridegroom holds his levée,
his numerous friends, and sympathy makes them
numerous on these happy occasions, pour in to

offer their congratulations. Abundance of refreshments of the most substantial kind, are
placed on side-tables, which are taken, not as
a formal meal, but as they walk up and down
the apartments, in cheerful conversation. This
running meal continues from noon till the close
of the evening, the bride never making her
appearance on the occasion ; an example of
delicacy worthy the imitation of more refined
societies.

June 28. Cincinnati. The Merino mania seems
to have prevailed in America to a degree exceeding its highest pitch in England. In Kentucky, where even the negroes would no more
eat mutton than they would horse-flesh, there
were great Merino breeders. There was and
is, I believe, a sheep society here, to encourage
the growth of fine wool, on land as rich as the
deepest, fattest vallies of our island, and in a
country still overwhelmed with timber of the
heaviest growth. As strange and incomprehensible an infatuation this; and as inconsistent
with plain common sense, as the determined
rejection of the fine-woolled race by the English
breeders of short-woolled sheep: but that
there should ever have been a rage for sheep
of any kind in any part of this country that I
have seen, must be owing to general ignorance
of the constitution and habits of this animal.

There is not a district, scarcely a spot that I have travelled over, where a flock of fine-woolled sheep could be kept with any prospect of advantage, provided there were even a market for the carcase. Yet by the ragged remains of the Merino family, which may be recognized in many places, I perceive that the attempt has been very general. Mutton is almost as abhorrent to an American palate, or fancy, as the flesh of swine to an Israelite; and the state of the manufactures does not give great encouragement to the growth of wool of any kind;—of Merino wool less, perhaps, than any other. Mutton is sold, in the markets of Philadelphia, at about half the price of beef; and the Kentuckian, who would have given a thousand dollars for a Merino ram, would dine upon dry bread, rather than taste his own mutton! A few sheep on every farm, to supply coarse wool for domestic manufacture, seems to be all that ought at present to be attempted, in any part of America that I have yet seen.

I have heard, that in the western part of Virginia, sheep are judiciously treated, and kept to advantage, and that there exists in that country no prejudice against the meat: also that the north-eastern state have good sheep pastures, and a *moderate* dislike of mutton: to

these, of course, my remarks on sheep-husban-
dry, are not applicable. Deep woods are not
the proper abodes of sheep.

When America shall have cleared away her
forests, and opened her uplands to the breezes,
they will soon be covered with fine turf, and
flocks will be seen ranging over them here, as
in other parts of the world. Anticipation often
retards improvement, by giving birth to prejudice.

There are about two thousand people regularly employed as boatmen on the Ohio, and they
are proverbially ferocious and abandoned in their
habits, though with many exceptions, as I have
good grounds for believing. People who settle
along the line of this grand navigation, generally possess or acquire similar habits ; and
thus, profligacy of manners seems inseparable
from the population on the banks of these great
rivers. It is remarked, indeed, every where,
that inland navigators are worse than sailors.

This forms a material objection to a residence
on the Ohio : outweighing all the beauty and
local advantages of such a situation.

July 6. We are now at the town of Madison,
on our way through the state of Indiana, towards
Vincennes. This place is on the banks of the
Ohio, about seventy-five miles from Cincinnati.

Our road has been mostly from three to six

miles from the river, passing over fertile hills, and alluvial bottoms.

The whole is appropriated; but although settlements multiply daily, many large intervals remain between the clearings.

Indiana is evidently newer than the state of Ohio; and if I mistake not, the character of the settlers is different, and superior to that of the first settlers in Ohio, who were generally very indigent people: those who are now fixing themselves in Indiana, bring with them habits of comfort, and the means of procuring the conveniences of life: I observe this in the construction of their cabins, and the neatness surrounding them, and especially in their well-stocked gardens, so frequent here, and so rare in the state of Ohio, where their earlier and longer settlement would have afforded them better opportunities of making this great provision for domestic comfort.

I have also had the pleasure of seeing many families of healthy children; and from my own continued observation, confirmed by the testimony of every competent evidence that has fallen in my way, I repeat with still more confidence, that the diseases so alarming to all emigrants, and which have been fatal to so many, are not attached to the climate, but to local situation. Repetitions will be excused on this important subject. Hills on a dry soil are healthy, after some progress has been made in clearing ; for deep and close woods are not salubrious either to new comers or old settlers. The neighbourhood of overflowing streams, and all wet, marshy soils, are productive of agues and bilious fevers in the autumn.

Such is the influx of strangers into this state, that the industry of the settlers is severely taxed to provide food for themselves, and a superfluity for new comers : and thus it is probable there will be a market for all the spare produce, for a series of years, owing to the accession of strangers, as well as the rapid internal growth of population. This is a favourable condition of a new colony, which has not been calculated on by those who take a distinct view of the subject. This year Kentucky has sent a supply in aid of this hungry infant state.

July 7. I have good authority for contradicting a supposition that I have met with in England, respecting the inhabitants of Indiana; —that they are lawless, semi-barbarous vagabonds, dangerous to live among. On the contrary, the laws are respected, and are effectual ; and the manners of the people are kind and gentle, to each other, and to strangers.

An unsettled country, lying contiguous to one that is settled, is always a place of retreat for rude and even abandoned characters, who find the regulations of society intolerable ; and such, no doubt, had taken up their unfixed abode in Indiana. These people retire, with the wolves, from the regular colonists, keeping always to the outside of civilized settlements. They rely for their subsistence on their rifle, and a scanty cultivation of corn, and live in great poverty and privation, a degree only short of the savage state of Indians.

Of the present settlers, as I have passed along, from house to house, I could not avoid receiving a most favourable impression. I would willingly remain among them, but pre-occupation sends us still forward in the steps of the roaming hunters I have just described, some of whom we shall probably dislodge, when we make our settlement, which, like theirs, will probably be in the confines of society.

As to the inhabitants of towns, the Ameri-cans are much alike, as far as we have had an opportunity of judging. We look, in vain, for any striking difference in the general deport-ment and appearance of the great bulk of Ame-ricans, from Norfolk on the eastern coast, to the town of Madison in Indiana. The same good-looking, well-dressed (not what we call gentle-manly) men appear every where. Nine out of ten, native Americans, are tall and long-limbed,

approaching, or even exceeding six feet; in
pantaloons and Wellington boots, either march-
ing up and down with their hands in their
pockets, or seated on chairs poised on the hind-
feet, and the backs rested against the walls.
If a hundred Americans of any class were to
seat themselves, ninety-nine would shuffle their
chairs to the true distance, and then throw
themselves back against the nearest prop. The
women exhibit a great similarity of tall relaxed
forms, with consistent dress and demeanour;
and are not remarkable for sprightliness of
manners. Intellectual culture has not yet made
much progress among the generality of either
sex where I have travelled; but the men have
greatly the advantage in the means of acquiring
information, from the habits of travelling, and
intercourse with strangers: — sources of improvement from which the other sex is unhappily too much secluded.

Lexington. This town is only three years
old. Madison dates its origin two years farther
back. Yet, much as has been done during this
short period, and much as there remains to do,
we see in every village and town, as we pass
along, groups of young able-bodied men, who
seem to be as perfectly at leisure as the loungers
of ancient Europe. This love of idleness where
labour is so profitable and effective, is a strange

affection. I have no notion of life as a pleasurable thing, except where connected with action. Rest is certainly a delightful sensation, but it implies previous labour : there is no rest for the indolent, any more than for the wicked : " They yawn and stretch, but find no rest."—I suspect, that indolence is the epidemic evil of the Americans. If you enquire of hale young fellows, why they remain in this listless state—" We live in freedom," they say, " we need not work like the English." Thus they consider it their privilege to do nothing. But the trees of the forest are still more highly privileged in this sort of passive existence; this living to do nothing ; for they are fed and exercised without any toil at *all*; the trees, " *sua si bona norint*," did they but know their bliss, might be objects of envy to many a tall young American.

July 12. Hawkins' Tavern, sixteen miles east of Vincennes. On traversing the state of Indiana to this place, I retain the same idea as to the character of the settlers that struck me on our entrance. They are an order of colonists somewhat higher than the first settlers of their sister state. There remains, however, a considerable number of backwoods' men, somewhat savage in character, and who look on new comers as intruders. The accommodation for travellers will soon be greatly superior to those in the

Ohio state, as are those of the Ohio to the taverns of Pennsylvania, west of the mountains.

The country, from the town of Madison, to the Camp Tavern, is not interesting, and great part of it is but of medium quality. At the latter place commences a broken country, approaching to mountainous, which, if well watered, would form a fine grazing district; but the little streams are now dried up, notwithstanding the late copious rains. This beautiful country continues as far as Sholt's Tavern, on White River, thirty-six miles east of Vincennes. Most of this hilly district is unentered, and remains open to the public at two dollars per acre.

Our rear party, consisting of one of the ladies, a servant boy, and myself, were benighted, in consequence of accidental detention, at the foot of one of these rugged hills; and without being well provided, were compelled to make our first experiment of " camping out."

A traveller in the woods should always carry flint, steel, tinder, and matches, a few biscuits, a half-pint phial of spirits, and a tin cup, a large knife or tomahawk; then with his two blankets, and his great coat, and umbrella, he need not be uneasy, should any unforeseen delay require his sleeping under a tree.

Our party having separated, the important articles of tinder and matches were in the baggage of the division which had proceeded, and as the night was rainy and excessively dark, we were for some time under some anxiety least we should have been deprived of the comfort and security of a fire. Fortunately, my powder-flask was in my saddle-bags, and we succeeded in supplying the place of tinder, by moistening a piece of paper, and rubbing it with gun-powder. We placed our touch-paper on an old cambric handkerchief, as the most readily combustible article in our stores. On this we scattered gunpowder pretty copiously, and our flint and steel soon enabled us to raise a flame, and collecting dry wood, we made a noble fire. There was a mattrass for the lady, a bear-skin for myself, and the load of the packhorse as a pallet for the boy. Thus, by means of great coats, and blankets, and our umbrellas spread over our heads, we made our quarters comfortable, and placing ourselves to the lee-ward of the fire, with our feet towards it, we lay more at ease than in the generality of taverns. Our horses fared rather worse, but we took care to tie them where they could browse a little, and occasionally shifted their quarters. We had a few biscuits, a small bottle of spirits, and a phial of oil: with the latter we contrived, by twisting some twine very hard, and dipping it in the oil, to make torches; and after several fruitless attempts we succeeded in finding water; we also collected plenty of dry wood. "Camping out" when the tents are pitched by daylight, and the party is ready furnished with the articles which we were obliged to supply by expedients, is quite pleasant in fine weather : my companion was exceedingly ill, which was in fact, the cause of our being benighted ; and never was the night's charge of a sick friend undertaken with more dismal forebodings, especially during our ineffectual efforts to obtain fire, the first blaze of which was unspeakably delightful : after this, the rain ceased, and the invalid passed the night in safety ; so that the morning found us more comfortable than we could have anticipated.

It has struck me as we have passed along from one poor hut to another among the rude inhabitants of this infant state, that travellers in general, who judge by comparison, are not qualified to form a fair estimate of these lonely settlers. Let a stranger make his way through England, in a course remote from the great roads, and going to no inns, take such entertainment only as he might find in the cottages of labourers, he would have as much cause to complain of the rudeness of the people, and far more of their drunkenness and profligacy than in these backwoods, although in England the poor are a part of a society where institutions are matured by the experience of two thousand years. The bulk of the inhabitants of this vast wilderness may be fairly considered as of the class of the lowest English peasantry, or just emerging from it : but in their manners and morals, and especially in their knowledge and proud independence of mind, they exhibit a contrast so striking, that he must indeed be a *petit maitre* traveller, or ill-informed of the character and circumstances of his poor countrymen, or deficient in good and manly sentiment, who would not rejoice to transplant, into these boundless regions of freedom, the millions whom he has left behind him, grovelling in ignorance and want.

Vincennes, July 13. The town is scattered over a plain, lying some feet lower than the banks of the Wabash :—a situation seemingly unfavourable to health ; and in fact, agues and bilious fevers are frequent in the autumn.

The road from Sholt's Tavern to this place, thirty-six miles, is partly across " barrens," that is, land of middling quality, thinly set with timber, or covered with long grass and shrubby underwood; generally level and dry, and gaudy with marigolds, sunflowers, martagon lilies, and many other brilliant flowers ; small " prairies," which are grass lands, free from underwood, and generally somewhat marshy; and rich bottom land: on the whole, the country is tame, poorly watered, and not desirable as a place of settlement: but it is pleasant to travel over from its varied character.

Vincennes exhibits a motly assemblage of inhabitants as well as visitors. The inhabitants are Americans, French, Canadians, Negroes; the visitors, among whom our party is conspicuous as English, (who are seldom seen in these parts,) Americans from various states, and Indians of various nations,—Shawnees, Delawares, and Miamies, who live about a hundred miles to the northward, and who are come here to trade for skins. The Indians are encamped in considerable numbers round the town, and are continually riding in, to the stores and the whiskey shops. Their horses and accoutrements are generally mean, and their persons disagreeable. Their faces are painted in various ways, which mostly gives a ferocity to their aspects.

One of them, a Shawnee, whom we met a few miles east of Vincennes, had his eyes, or rather his eyelids, and surrounding parts, daubed with vermillion, looking hideous enough at a distance, but on a nearer view, he has good features, and is a fine, stout, fierce looking man, well remembered at Vincennes for the trouble he gave during the late war. This man exhibits a respectable beard ; enough for a Germanized British officer of dragoons. Some of them are well dressed and good-looking people: one young man in particular, of the Miami nation, had a clear light blue cotton vest with sleeves, and his head ornamented with black feathers.

They all wear pantaloons or rather long mocassins of buckskin, covering the foot and leg, and reaching half way up the thigh which is bare: a covering of cloth, passing between the thighs and hanging behind, like an apron, of a foot square. Their complexion is various ; some dark, others not so swarthy as myself; but I saw none of the copper colour which I had imagined to be their universal distinctive mark. They are addicted to spirits and often intoxicated, but even then generally civil and good humoured. The Indians are said to be partial to the French traders ; thinking them fairer than the English or Americans. They use much action in their discourse, and laugh immoderately. Their hair is straight and black, and their eyes dark. The women are, many of them, decently dressed and good-looking ; they ride sometimes like the men, but side-saddles are not uncommon among them. Few of them of either sex speak English ; but many of the people here speak a variety of the Indian languages.

In the interior of the Illinois, the Indians are said sometimes to be troublesome, by giving abusive language to travellers, and stealing their horses when they encamp in the woods; but they never commit personal outrage.— Watchful dogs and a rifle, are the best security: but I believe we shall have no reason to fear interruption in the quarter to which we are going.

At this remote place we find ourselves in a comfortable tavern and surrounded by genteel and agreeable people. Our company at supper was about thirty.

The health of our party has been a source of some anxiety, increasing as the summer advances: as yet we have entirely escaped the diseases to which the country or climate, or both, are said to be liable ; but our approach to the Wabash has not been without some painful forebodings.

We have remarked, *en passant*, that people generally speak favourably of their own country, and exaggerate every objection or evil, when speaking of those to which we are going: thus it may be that the accounts we have received of the unhealthiness of this river and its vicinity, have been too deeply coloured. We are accordingly greatly relieved by the information we have received here on this subject. The

Wabash has not overflowed its banks this summer, and no apprehensions are now entertained,
as to the sickly season of August and September.

July 18. Princeton.—We, in Great Britain,
are so circumscribed in our movements that
miles with us seem equal to tens in America. I
believe that travellers here, will start on an expedition of three thousand miles by boats, on
horseback or on foot, with as little deliberation
or anxiety, as we should set out on a journey of
three hundred.

Five hundred persons every summer pass down
the Ohio from Cincinnati to New Orleans, as
traders or boatmen, and return on foot. By
water, the distance is seventeen hundred miles,
and the walk back a thousand. Many go down
to New Orleans from Pittsburg, which adds
five hundred miles to the distance by water, and
three hundred by land. The store-keepers,
(country shopkeepers we should call them) of
these western towns, visit the eastern ports of
Baltimore, New York and Philadelphia, once a
year, to lay in their stock of goods : an evidence
it might seem of want of confidence in the merchants of those places ; but the great variety of
articles, and the risk attending their carriage
to so great a distance, by land and water,
render it necessary that the store-keepers

should attend both to their purchase and conveyance.

I think the time is at hand when these periodical transmontane journeys are to give place to expeditions down the Ohio and Mississippi to New Orleans. The vast and increasing produce of these states, in grain, flour, cotton, sugar, tobacco, peltry, timber, &c. &c. which finds a ready vent at New Orleans, will be returned, through the same channel in the manufactures of Europe and the luxuries of the east, to supply the growing demands of this western world. How rapidly this demand actually increases, it is utterly impossible to estimate; but some idea of it may be formed from a general view of the cause and manners of its growth. In round numbers there are probably half a million of inhabitants in Ohio, Indiana and Illinois. Immigration (if I may be allowed to borrow a new but good word,) and births, will probably double this number in about six years; and in the mean time, the prosperous circumstances of almost every family, are daily creating new wants, and awakening fresh necessities.

On any spot where a few settlers cluster together, attracted by ancient neighbourhood, or by the goodness of the soil, or vicinity to a mill, or by whatever cause, some enterprising proprietor finds in his section what he deems a good scite for a town : he has it surveyed and laid out in lots, which he sells, or offers for sale by auction.

The new town then assumes the name of its founder :—a store-keeper builds a little framed store, and sends for a few cases of goods ; and then a tavern starts up, which becomes the residence of a doctor and a lawyer, and the boarding-house of the store-keeper, as well as the resort of the weary traveller : soon follow a blacksmith and other handicraftsmen in useful succession : a schoolmaster, who is also the minister of religion, becomes an important accession to this rising community. Thus the town proceeds, if it proceeds at all, with accumulating force, until it becomes the metropolis of the neighbourhood. Hundreds of these speculations may have failed, but hundreds prosper ; and thus trade begins and thrives, as population grows around these lucky spots ; imports and exports maintaining their just proportion. One year ago the neighbourhood of this very town of Princeton, was clad in " buckskin ;" now the men appear at church in good blue cloth, and the women in fine calicoes and straw bonnets.

The town being fairly established, a cluster of inhabitants, small as it may be, acts as a stimulus on the cultivation of the neighbourhood :

redundancy of supply is the consequence, and this demands a vent. Water mills, or in defect of water power, steam mills rise on the nearest navigable stream, and thus an effectual and constant market is secured for the increasing surplus of produce. Such are the elements of that accumulating mass of commerce, in exports, and consequent imports, which will render the Mississippi the greatest thoroughfare in the world.

At Vincennes, the foundation is just laid of a large establishment of mills to be worked by steam. Water mills of great power are now building on the Wabash, near Harmony, and undertakings of a similar kind will be called for and executed all along this river, which, with its tributary rivers, several of which are also navigable, from the east and the west, is the outlet of a very rich and thickly settling country, comprising the prime of Indiana, and a valuable portion of the Illinois, over the space of about one hundred thousand square miles.

There is nothing in Vincennes, on its first appearance to make a favourable impression on a stranger ; but it improves on acquaintance, for it contains agreeable people ; and there is a spirit of cleanliness, and even neatness in their houses and manner of living : there is also a strain of politeness, which marks the origin of this settlement in a way which is very flattering to the French.

It is a phenomenon in national character which I cannot explain; but the fact will not be disputed, that the urbanity of manners which distinguishes that nation from all others, is never entirely lost; but that French politeness remains until every trace of French origin is obliterated. A Canadian Frenchman who, after having spent twenty years of his prime among the Indians, settles in the backwoods of the United States, still retains a strong impression of French good breeding.

Is it by this attractive qualification that the French have obtained such sway among the Indians? I think it may be attributed with as much probability to their conciliating manner, as to superior integrity; though the latter has been the cause generally assigned.

This tenaciousness of national character, under all changes of climate and circumstances, of which the French afford many remarkable instances, is the more curious, as it is not universal among nations, though the Germans afford, I am told, examples equally strong. This country gives favourable opportunities for observation on this interesting subject.

What is it that distinguishes an Englishman from other men? or is there any mark of national character, which neither time, climate, nor circumstances can obliterate? An anglo-American is not English, but a German is a German, and a Frenchman French, to the fourth, perhaps to the tenth generation.

The Americans have no central focus of fashion, or local standard of politeness; therefore remoteness can never be held as an apology for sordid dress or coarse demeanour. They are strangers to rural simplicity: the embarrassed air of an awkward rustic, so frequent in England, is rarely seen in the United States. This no doubt, is the effect of political equality, the consciousness of which accompanies all their intercourse, and may be supposed to operate most powerfully on the manners of the lowest class: for high and low there are, and will be, even here, and in every society, from causes moral and physical, which no political regulations can or ought to controul.

In viewing the Americans, and sketching, in a rude manner, as I pass along, their striking characteristics, I have seen a deformity so general that I canot help esteeming it national, though I know it admits of very many individual exceptions. I have written it and then erased it, wishing to pass it by: but it won't do:—it is the truth, and to the truth I must adhere. Cleanliness in houses and too often in person, is neglected to a degree which is very revolting to an Englishman.

America was bred in a cabin : this is not a reproach ; for the origin is most honourable : but as she has exchanged her hovel of unhewn logs for a framed building, and that again for a mansion of brick, some of her cabin habits have been unconsciously retained. Many have already been quitted ; and, one by one, they will all be cleared away, as I am told they are now in the cities of the eastern states.

There are, I believe, court-houses, which are also made use of as places of worship, in which filth of all kinds have been accumulating ever since they were built. What reverence can be felt for the majesty of religion, or of the laws, in such sties of abomination ? The people who are content to assemble in them can scarcely respect each other.—Here is a bad public example. It is said, that to clean these places is the office of no one —But why is no person appointed? Might it not be inferred that a disregard to the decencies of life prevails through such a community ?

July 19. We are at Princeton, in a log tavern, where neatness is as well observed as at many taverns in the city of Bath, or any city. The town will soon be three years old ; the people belong to old America in dress and manners, and would not disgrace old England in the general decorum of their deportment.

But I lament here, as every where, the small account that is had of time. Subsistence is secured so easily, and liberal pursuits being yet too rare to operate as a general stimulus to exertion, life is whiled away in a painful state of yawning lassitude.

July 20. The object of our pursuit, like the visions of fancy, has hitherto seemed to recede from our approach: we are, however, at length, arrived at the point where reality is likely to reward our labours.

Twenty or thirty miles west of this place, in the Illinois territory, is a large country where settlements are just now beginning; and where there is abundant choice of unentered lands of a description which will satisfy our wishes, if the statements of travellers and surveyors can be relied on, after great abatements.

This is a critical season of the year, and we feel some anxiety for the health of our party, consisting of ten individuals. July, and the two succeeding months, are trying to the constitutions of new comers, and this danger must be incurred by us; we hope, however, under circumstances of great mitigation. In the first place, the country is at present, free from sickness, and the floods were too early in the spring, to occasion any apprehensions of an unhealthy autumn to the inhabitants. In the next place, we have an opportunity of choice of situation for our temporary sojourn. Unfortunately, this opportunity of choice is limited by the scarcity of houses, and the indifference evinced by settlers to the important object of health, in the fixing their own habitations. The vicinity of rivers from the advantages of navigation and machinery, as well as the fertility of soil having generally suspended a proper solicitude about health.

Prince Town affords a situation for a temporary abode, more encouraging than any place we have before visited in this neighbourhood : it stands on an elevated spot, in an uneven or rolling country, ten miles from the Wabash, and two from the navigable stream of the Patok : but the country is very rich, and the timber vast in bulk and height, so that though healthy at present, to its inhabitants, they can hardly encourage us with the hope of escaping the seasoning to which they say all new comers are subject. There is a very convenient house to be let for nine months, for which we are in treaty. This will accommodate us until our own be prepared for our reception in the spring, and may be rented, with a garden well stocked, for about £20. I think we shall engage it, and, should a sickly season come on, recede for a time into the high country, about a hundred miles back, returning here to winter, when the danger is past.

As to travelling in the backwoods of America, I think there is none so agreeable, after you have used yourself to repose in your own pallet, either on the floor of a cabin, or under the canopy of the woods, with an umbrella over your head, and a noble fire at your feet: you will then escape the only serious nuisance of American travelling—viz. hot rooms and swarming beds, exceeding, instead of repairing, the fatigues of the day. Some difficulties occur from ferries, awkward fords, and rude bridges, with occasional swamps; but such is the sagacity and sure-footedness of the horses, that accidents happen very rarely.

July 21. This is an efficient government. It seems that some irregularities exist, or are suspected in the proceedings of certain of the offices which are established for the sale of public lands. Whilst we were at Vincennes, a confidential individual from the federal city made his appearance at the land office there, with authority to inspect and examine on the spot. Last night the same gentleman lodged here, on his way to the land office at Shawnee Town, at which we propose to make our entries, where he is equally unexpected as he had been at Vincennes, and where his visit is somewhat *mal-a-propos* as to our convenience. One of the efficient officers, the register, had been left by us sick, about seventy miles from Cincinnati, and the other, the receiver, passed this place for Vincennes yesterday, and fixed to return on Sunday, in order to proceed with me through the woods, on Monday, on an exploring expedition to the Illinois. The republican delegate informed me immediately on his arrival, that he had left an absolute injunction for the instant return of the receiver to his office, expressing regret at deranging my plans, at the same time making ample amends by his own arrangement for my accommodation.

The effect produced at Vincennes under my observation, and the decided manner of this gentleman, convince me that this mode of treatment is fully as effectual as that by "motion for the production of papers and committees for their examination," by which deliberate procedure the inconvenience of surprise is politely obviated.

July 23. The small-pox is likely to be excluded from this state, vaccination being very generally adopted, and inoculation for the small-pox prohibited altogether,—not by law, but by common consent. If it should be known that an individual had undergone the operation, the inhabitants would compel him to withdraw entirely from society.—If he lived in a town, he must absent himself, or he would be driven off.

Mental derangement is nearly unknown in these new countries. There is no instance of insanity at present in this state, which probably, now contains 100,000 inhabitants. A middle-aged man, of liberal attainments and observation, who has lived much of his life in Kentucky, and has travelled a good deal over the western country, remarked, as an incident of extraordinary occurrence, that he once knew a lady afflicted with this malady.

The simple maxim, that a man has a right to do any thing but injure his neighbour, is very broadly adopted into the practical as well as political code of this country.

A good citizen is the common designation of respect, when a man speaks of his neighbour as a virtuous man—" he is a very good citizen."

Drunkenness is rare, and quarrelling rare in proportion. Personal resistance to personal aggression, or designed affront, holds a high place in the class of duties with the citizens of Indiana.

It seems that the Baptists, (who are the prevailing sect in this country,) by their religious tenets, would restrain this summary mode of redressing injuries among the brethren of their

church : a respectable but knotty member of
that community was lately arraigned before
their spiritual tribunal for supporting heterodox
opinions on this subject. After hearing the argu-
ments derived from the texts of scripture, which
favour the doctrine of non-resistance, he rose,
and with energy of action suited to his words,
declared that he should not wish to live longer
than he had the right to knock down the man
who told him he lied.

July 24. Regretting, as I must, my perpetual
separation from many with whom I was in
habits of agreeable intercourse in old England,
I am much at my ease on the score of society.
We shall possess this one thing needful, which
it was supposed the wilderness could not supply, in the families of our own establishment,
and a circle of citizen neighbours, such as this
little town affords already. There prevails so
much good sense and useful knowledge, joined
to a genuine warmth of friendly feeling, a disposition to promote the happiness of each other,
that the man who is lonely among them is not
formed for society. Such are the citizens of these
new states, and my unaffected and well considered wish is to spend among them the remainder of my days.

The social compact here is not the confe-
deracy of a few to reduce the many into subjec-

tion ; but is indeed, and in truth, among these simple republicans, a combination of talents, moral and physical, by which the good of all is promoted in perfect accordance with individual interest. It is, in fact, a better, because a more simple state than was ever pourtrayed by an Utopian theorist.

But the people, like their fellow men, have their irregular and rude passions, and their gross propensities and follies ; suited to their condition, as weeds to a particular soil : so that this, after all, is the real world, and no poetical Arcadia.

One agreeable fact, characteristic of these young associations, presses more and more upon my attention :—there is a great amount of social feeling, much real society in new countries, compared with the number of inhabitants. Their importance to each other on many interesting occasions creates kind sentiments. They have fellow-feeling in hope and fear, in difficulty and success, and they make ten-fold more of each other than the crowded inhabitants of populous countries.

July 25. Harmony. Yesterday we explored the country from this place to the Ohio, about eighteen miles, and returned to-day by a different route. There is a great breadth of valuable land vacant; not the extremely rich river-bottom land, but close, cool sand of excellent quality. It is, however, not so well watered, nor so much varied in surface as is desirable ; and we are so taken with the prairies we have seen, and with the accounts we have heard of those before us in the Illinois, that no " timbered" land can satisfy our present views.

We lodged last night in a cabin at a very new town, called Mount Vernon, on the banks of the Ohio. Here we found the people of a cast confirming my aversion to a settlement in the immediate vicinity of a large navigable river. Every hamlet is demoralized, and every plantation is liable to outrage, within a short distance of such a thoroughfare.

Yet, the view of that noble expanse was like the opening of bright day upon the gloom of night, to us who had been so long buried in deep forests. It is a feeling of confinement, which begins to damp the spirits, from this complete exclusion of distant objects. To travel day after day, among trees of a hundred feet high, without a glimpse of the surrounding country, is oppressive to a degree which those cannot conceive who have not experienced it; and it must depress the spirits of the solitary settler to pass years in this state. His visible horizon extends no farther than the tops of the trees which bound his plantation—perhaps, five hundred yards. Upwards he sees the sun and sky, and stars, but around him an eternal forest, from which he can never hope to emerge :—not so in a thickly settled district ; he cannot there enjoy any freedom of prospect, yet there is variety, and some scope for the imprisoned vision. In a hilly country a little more range of view may occasionally be obtained; and a river is a stream of light as well as of water, which feasts the eye with a delight inconceivable to the inhabitants of open countries.

Under these impressions a prairie country increases in attraction ; and to-morrow we shall commence a round in the Illinois, which we hope will enable us to take some steps towards our final establishment.

July 26. Left Harmony after breakfast, and crossing the Wabash at the ferry, three miles below, we proceeded to the Big-Prairie, where, to our astonishment, we beheld a fertile plain of grass and arable, and some thousand acres covered with corn, more luxuriant than any we had before seen. The scene reminded us of some open, well cultivated vale in Europe, surrounded by wooded uplands ; and forgetting that we were, in fact, on the very frontiers, beyond which few settlers had penetrated, we were transported in idea to the fully peopled regions we had left so far behind us.

On our arrival at Mr. Williams' habitation,

the illusion vanished : though the owner of an
estate in this prairie, on which at this time are
nearly three hundred acres of beautiful corn in
one field, he lives in a way, apparently, as remote
from comfort, as the settler of one year, who
thinks only of the means of supporting existence.

We had also an opportunity of seeing the
youth of the neighbourhood, as the muster of the
militia took place this day at his house. The
company amounts to about thirty, of whom
about twenty attended with their rifles. In per-
forming the exercise, which was confined to the
handling their arms, they were little adroit ; but
in the use of them against an invading foe, woe
to their antagonists!

The soil of the Big-Prairie, which is of no
great extent, notwithstanding its name, is a
rich cool sand ; that is to say, one of the most
desirable description. It extends about five
miles by four, bounded by an irregular outline of
lofty timber, like a lake of verdure, most cheering
to our eyes, just emerging from the dark woods
of Indiana : this prairie is somewhat marshy, and
there is much swampy ground between it and
the Wabash, which is distant seven miles : the
settlers have, in consequence, suffered from
ague and other bilious complaints, but they are
now much more healthy than they were on the

first settlement. Cultivation seems to alter the character of the soil : where the plough goes it is no longer a marsh, but dry sandy arable. About thirty miles to the north of this, which was among the earliest prairie settlements of the district, (having been done four or five years) there are prairies of higher aspect, and uneven surface, to which our attention is directed, we found a few settlers round one of these, who are now watching their first crop.

These people are healthy, and the females and children better complexioned than their neighbours of the timber country. It is evident that they breathe better air : but they are in a low state of civilization, about half-Indian in their mode of life : they also seem to have less cordiality towards a " land hunter," as they with some expression of contempt, call the stranger who explores their country in quest of a home.

Their habits of life do not accord with those of a thickly settled neighbourhood : they are hunters by profession, and they would have the whole range of the forests for themselves and their cattle.—Thus strangers appear among them as invaders of their privileges ; as *they* have intruded on the better founded, exclusive privileges of their Indian predecessors.

But there are agreeable exceptions to the

coarse part of this general character. I have
met with pleasant intelligent people who were
a perfect contrast to their semi-Indian neighbours; cleanly, industrious, and orderly; whilst
ignorance, indolence, and disorder, with a total
disregard of cleanliness in their houses and
persons are too characteristic of the hunter tribe.

August 1. Dagley's, twenty miles north of
Shawnee Town. After viewing several beautiful prairies, so beautiful with their surrounding
woods as to seem like the creation of fancy, gardens of delight in a dreary wilderness ; and
after losing our horses and spending two days
in recovering them, we took a hunter as our
guide, and proceeded across the Little Wabash, to explore the country between that river
and the Skillet-fork.

Since we left the Fox settlement, about fifteen
miles north of the Big-Prairie, cultivation has
been very scanty, many miles intervening between the little " clearings." This may therefore be truly called, a new country.

These lonely settlers are poorly off ;—their
bread corn must be ground thirty miles off, requiring three days to carry to the mill, and bring
back, the small horse-load of three bushels.
Articles of family manufacture are very scanty,
and what they purchase is of the meanest quality and excessively dear : yet they are friendly

and willing to share their simple fare with you. It is surprising how comfortable they seem, wanting every thing. To struggle with privations has now become the habit of their lives, most of them having made several successive plunges into the wilderness ; and they begin already to talk of selling their " improvements," and getting farther " back," on finding that emigrants of another description are thickening about them.

Our journey across the Little Wabash was a complete departure from all mark of civilization. We saw no bears, as they are now buried in the thickets, and seldom appear by day ; but, at every few yards, we saw recent marks of their doings, " wallowing" in the long grass, or turning over the decayed logs in quest of beetles or worms, in which work the strength of this animal is equal to that of four men. Wandering without track, where even the sagacity of our hunter-guide had nearly failed us, we at length arrived at the cabin of another hunter, where we lodged.

This man and his family are remarkable instances of the effect on the complexion, produced by the perpetual incarceration of a thorough woodland life. Incarceration may seem to be a term less applicable to the condition of a roving backwoods' man than to any other, and especially unsuitable to the habits of this individual and his family; for the cabin in which he entertained us, is the third dwelling he has built within the last twelve months; and a very slender motive would place him in a fourth before the ensuing winter. In his general habits, the hunter ranges as freely as the beasts he pursues: labouring under no restraint, his activity is only bounded by his own physical powers: still he is incarcerated—" Shut from the common air." Buried in the depth of a boundless forest, the breeze of health never reaches these poor wanderers; the bright prospect of distant hills fading away into the semblance of clouds, never cheered their sight: they are tall and pale, like vegetables that grow in a vault, pining for light.

The man, his pregnant wife, his eldest son, a tall half-naked youth, just initiated in the hunters' arts, his three daughters, growing up into great rude girls, and a squalling tribe of dirty brats of both sexes, are of one pale yellow, without the slightest tint of healthful bloom.

In passing through a vast expanse of the backwoods, I have been so much struck with this effect, that I fancy I could determine the colour of the inhabitants, if I was apprised of the depth of their immersion; and, *vice versa*, I could judge of the extent of the " clearing" if

I saw the people. The blood, I fancy, is not supplied with its proper dose of oxygen from their gloomy atmosphere, crowded with vegetables growing almost in the dark, or decomposing; and, in either case, abstracting from the air this vital principle.

Our stock of provisions being nearly exhausted, we were anxious to provide ourselves with a supper by means of our guns; but we could meet with neither deer nor turkey; however, in our utmost need, we shot three racoons, an old one to be roasted for our dogs, and the two young ones to be stewed up daintily for ourselves. We soon lighted a fire, and cooked the old racoon for the dogs; but, famished as they were, they would not touch it, and their squeamishness so far abated our relish for the promised stew, that we did not press our complaining landlady to prepare it: and thus our supper consisted of the residue of our "corn" bread, and *no* racoon. However, we laid our bearskins on the filthy earth, (floor there was none,) which they assured us was "too damp for fleas," and wrapped in our blankets, slept soundly enough; though the collops of venison, hanging in comely rows in the smoky fire-place, and even the shoulders, put by for the dogs, and which were suspended over our heads, would have been an acceptable prelude to our night's rest, had we been invited to partake of them; but our hunter and our host were too deeply engaged in conversation to think of supper. In the morning the latter kindly invited us to cook some of the collops, which we did by toasting them on a stick; and he also divided some shoulders among the dogs:—so we all fared sumptuously.

The cabin, which may serve as a specimen of these rudiments of houses, was formed of round logs, with apertures of three or four inches between: no chimney, but large intervals between the "clapboards," for the escape of the smoke. The roof was, however, a more effectual covering than we have generally experienced, as it protected us very tolerably from a drenching night. Two bedsteads of unhewn logs, and cleft boards laid across;—two chairs, one of them without a bottom, and a low stool, were all the furniture required by this numerous family. A string of buffalo hide, stretched across the hovel, was a wardrobe for their rags; and their utensils, consisting of a large iron pot, some baskets, the effective rifle and two that were superannuated, stood about in corners, and the fiddle, which was only silent when we were asleep, hung by them.

Our racoons, though lost to us and our hungry dogs, furnished a new set of strings for this favourite instrument. Early in the morning the youth had made good progress in their preparation, as they were cleaned and stretched on a tree to dry.

Many were the tales of dangerous adventures in their hunting expeditions, which kept us from our pallets till a late hour; and the gloomy morning allowed our hunters to resume their discourse, which no doubt would have been protracted to the evening, had not our impatience to depart caused us to interrupt it, which we effected, with some difficulty, by eleven in the forenoon.

These hunters are as persevering as savages, and as indolent. They cultivate indolence as a privilege :—" You English are very industrious, but we have freedom." And thus they exist in yawning indifference, surrounded with nuisances, and petty wants, the first to be removed, and the latter supplied by a tenth of the time loitered away in their innumerable idle days.

Indolence, under various modifications, seems to be the easily besetting sin of the Americans, where I have travelled. The Indian probably stands highest on the scale, as an example; the backwoods' man the next; the new settler, who declines hunting takes a lower degree, and so on. I have seen interesting exceptions even among the hunting tribe; but the malady is a prevailing one in all classes :—I note it again, and again, not in the spirit of satire, but as a hint for reformation :

" To know ourselves diseas'd is half a cure."

The Little Wabash, which we crossed in search of some prairies, which had been described to us in glowing colours, is a sluggish and scanty stream at this season, but for three months of the latter part of winter and spring, it covers a great space by the overflow of waters collected in its long course. The Skillet-fork is also a river of similar character ; and the country lying between them must labour under the inconvenience of absolute seclusion for many months every year, until bridges and ferries are established : this would be a bar to our settling within the " Fork," as it is called : we therefore separated this morning, without losing the time that it would require to explore this part thoroughly I proceed to Shawnee Town land office, to make some entries which we had determined on, between the Little and the Big Wabash. Mr. Flower spends a day or two in looking about, and returns to our families at Princeton. Having made my way through this wildest of wildernesses to the Skillet-fork, 1 crossed it at a shoal, which affords a notable instance out of a thousand, of the utter worthlessness of reports about remote objects in this country, even from *soi-disant* eye-witnesses.

A grave old hunter, who had the air of much sagacity, declared to me, that he had visited this shoal, that it is a bed of limestone, a substance greatly wanting in this country. The son confirmed the father's account, adding, that he had seen the stone burnt into lime. It is micaceous sandstone slate, without the least affinity to lime-stone !

It is a dreadful country on each side of the Skillet-fork ; flat and swampy ; so that the water in many places, even at this season, renders travelling disagreeable ; yet here and there, at ten miles distance perhaps, the very solitude tempts some one of the family of Esau to pitch his tent for a season.

At one of these lone dwellings we found a neat, respectable-looking female, spinning under the little piazza at one side of the cabin, which shaded her from the sun : her husband was absent on business, which would detain him some weeks : she had no family, and no companion but her husband's faithful dog, which usually attended him in his bear hunting in the winter : she was quite overcome with "*lone*" she said, and hoped we would tie our horses in the wood, and sit awhile with her, during the heat of the day. We did so, and she rewarded us with a basin of coffee. Her husband was kind and good to her, and never left her without necessity, but a true lover of bear hunting; which he pursued alone, taking only his dog with him, though it is common for hunters to go in parties to attack this dangerous animal. He had killed a great number last winter; five, I think, in one week. The cabin of this hunter was neatly arranged, and the garden well stocked.

August 2. We lodged last night at another cabin, where similar neatness prevailed within and without. The woman neat, and the children clean in skin, and whole in their clothes. The man possessed of good sense and sound notions, ingenious and industrious, a contrast to backwoods' men in general. He lives on the edge of the seven miles' prairie, a spot charming to the eye, but deficient in surface-water; and they say the well-water is not good : I suppose they have not dug deeper than twenty-five feet, which is no criterion of the purity of springs in a soil absorbent from the surface to that depth.

Shawnee Town. This place I account as a phenomenon evincing the pertinacious adhesion of the human animal to the spot where it has once fixed itself. As the lava of Mount Etna cannot dislodge this strange being from the

cities which have been repeatedly ravaged by
its eruptions, so the Ohio with its annual over-
flowings is unable to wash away the inhabitants
of Shawnee Town.—Once a year, for a series of
successive springs, it has carried away the fences
from their cleared lands, till at length they have
surrendered, and ceased to cultivate them.
Once a year, the inhabitants either make their
escape to higher lands, or take refuge in their
upper stories, until the waters subside, when
they recover their position on this desolate sand-
bank.

Here is the land office for the south-east
district of Illinois, where I have just constituted
myself a land-owner by paying seven hundred
and twenty dollars, as one fourth of the purchase
money of fourteen hundred and forty acres:
this, with a similar purchase made by Mr.
Flower, is part of a beautiful and rich prairie,
about six miles distant from the Big, and the
same from the Little Wabash.

The land is rich natural meadow, bounded
by timbered land, within reach of two navigable rivers, and may be rendered immediately
productive at a small expence. The successful cultivation of several prairies has awakened
the attention of the public, and the value of
this description of land is now known; so that
the smaller portions, which are surrounded

by timber, will probably be settled so rapidly as to absorb, in a few months, all that is to be obtained at the government rate, of two dollars per acre.

Sand predominates in the soil of the south-eastern quarter of the Illinois territory:—the basis of the country is sand-stone, lying, I believe, on clay-slate. The bed of the Ohio, at Shawnee Town is sand-stone: forty miles north-east, near Harmony, is a quarry of the same stone, on the banks of the Big Wabash. The shoals of the Little Wabash and the Skillet-fork, twenty, forty, and sixty miles up, are of the same formation. No lime-stone has yet been discovered in the district. I have heard of coal in several places, but have not seen a specimen of it. Little, however, is yet known with precision of the surface of many parts of the country; and the wells, though numerous, rarely reach the depth of thirty feet, below which, I presume, the earth has in no instance been explored.

The geographical position of this portion of territory promises favourable for its future importance. The Big Wabash, a noble stream, forming its eastern boundary, runs a course of about four hundred miles, through one of the most fertile portions of this most fertile region. It has a communication well known to the Indian traders, with lake Huron and all the navigation of the north, by means of a portage of eight miles to the Miami of the lakes. This portage will, probably, be made navigable in a few years. Population is already very considerable along this river, and upon White River, another beautiful and navigable stream, which falls into the Wabash from the east. The Little Wabash, though a sluggish stream, is, or may become a navigable communication extending far north, I am *informed* four hundred miles.

The prairies have been represented as marshes, and many of them are so. This is not, however, the case with all. Our prairie rises at its northern extremity to a commanding height, being one of the most elevated portions of the country, surmounting and overlooking the woodlands to the south and west, to a great distance. There are also many others to the northward on lands of the same eligible character, high and fertile, and surrounded by timbered lands. These are unsurveyed, and of course are not yet offered to the public.

Nothing but fencing and providing water for stock is wanted to reduce a prairie into the condition of useful grass land ; and from that state, we all know, the transition to arable is through a simple process, easy to perform, and profitable as it goes on. Thus no addition, except the above on the score of improvement, is to be made to the first cost, as regards the land. Buildings, proportioned to the owner's inclination or purse, are of course requisite on every estate.

The dividing a section (six hundred and forty acres) into inclosures of twenty-five acres each, with proper avenues of communication, each inclosure being supplied with water, in the most convenient manner, and live hedges planted, or sown, will cost less than two dollars per acre. This, added to the purchase money, when the whole is paid, will amount to eighteen shillings sterling, per acre, or five hundred and seventy-six pounds for six hundred and forty acres.

Calculations on the capital to be employed, or expended on buildings, and stock alive and dead, would be futile, as this would be in proportion to the means. The larger the amount, within the limits of utility, the greater the profit: but, as the necessary outgoings are trifling, *a small sum will do.* Two thousand pounds sterling for these purposes would place the owner in a state of comfort, and even affluence.

I conclude from these data, that an English farmer possessing three thousand pounds, besides the charges of removal, may establish himself *well* as a proprietor and occupier of such an estate. The folly or the wisdom of the undertaking I leave among the propositions which are too plain to admit of illustration.

In their irregular outline of woodland and their undulating surface, these tracts of natural meadow exhibit every beauty, fresh from the hand of nature, which art often labours in vain to produce ; but there are no organs of perception, no faculties as yet prepared in this country, for the enjoyment of these exquisite combinations.

The grand in scenery I have been shocked to hear, by American lips, called disgusting, because the surface would be too rude for the plough ; and the epithet of *elegant* is used on every occasion of commendation but that to which it is appropriate in the English language.

An elegant improvement, is a cabin of rude logs, and a few acres with the trees cut down to the height of three feet, and surrounded by a worm-fence, or zig-zag railing. You hear of an *elegant* mill, an *elegant* orchard, an *elegant* tanyard, &c. and familiarly of *elegant* roads,—meaning such as you may pass without extreme peril. The word implies eligibility or usefulness in America, but has nothing to do with taste ; which is a term as strange to the American language, where I have heard it spoken, as comfort is said to be to the French, and for a similar reason :—the idea has not yet reached them. Nature has not yet displayed to them those charms of distant and various prospect, which will delight the future inhabitants of this noble country.

Scientific pursuits are also, generally speaking, unknown where I have travelled. Reading is very much confined to politics, history and poetry. Science is not, as in England, cultivated for its own sake. This is to be lamented the more, on account of the many heavy hours of indolence under which most people are doomed to toil, through every day of their existence. What yawning and stretching, and painful restlessness they would be spared, if their time were occupied in the acquisition of useful knowledge!

There is a sort of covetousness which would be the greatest of blessings, to those Americans whose circumstances excuse them from constant occupation for a subsistence,—that is, to the great majority of the people,—the covetousness of time, from a knowledge of its value.

The life and habits of the great Franklin, whose name, I am sorry to say, is not often heard here, would be a most profitable study. He possessed the true Philosopher's stone; for whatever he touched became gold under his hand, through the magical power of a scientific mind. This lamentable deficiency in science and taste, two such abundant sources of enjoyment, must not be attributed to a want of energy in the American character :—witness the spirit and good sense with which men of all ranks are seen to engage in discussions on politics, history, or religion ; subjects which have attracted, more or less, the attention of every one. Nature has done much for them, and they leave much to Nature : but they have made *themselves* free ;—this may account for their indifference to science, and their zeal in politics.

August 3. Harmony.—We left Shawnee Town this morning under more agreeable impressions regarding its inhabitants than we had entertained before we entered it. We found something, certainly, of river barbarism, the genuine Ohio character ; but we met with a greater number than we expected of agreeable individuals : these, and the kind and hospitable treatment we experienced at our tavern, formed a good contrast to the rude society and wretched fare we had left behind us at the Skillet-fork. At this, our third visit, Harmony becomes more enigmatical. This day, being Sunday, afforded us an opportunity of seeing grouped and in their best attire, a large part of the members of this wonderful community. It was evening

when we arrived, and we saw no human crea-
ture about the streets:—we had even to call
the landlord of the inn out of church to take
charge of our horses. The cows were waiting
round the little dwellings, to supply the inhabitants with their evening's meal. Soon the
entire body of people, which is about seven
hundred, poured out of the church, and exhi-
bited so much health, and peace, and neatness
in their persons, that we could not but exclaim,
surely the institutions which produce so much
happiness must have more of good than of evil
in them ; and here I rest, not lowered in my
abhorrence of the hypocrisy, if it be such, which
governs the ignorant by nursing them in superstition ; but inclined in charity to believe that
the leaders are sincere. Certain it is, that
living in such plenty, and a total abstraction
from care about the future provision for a
family, it must be some overbearing thraldom
that prevents an increase of their numbers by
the natural laws of population.

I had rather attribute this phenomenon to
bigotry pervading the mass, than charge a few
with the base policy of chaining a multitude,
by means of superstition. It is, however, difficult to separate the idea of policy from a con-
trivance which is so highly political. The
number of Mr. Rapp's *associates* would increase

so rapidly, without some artificial restraint, as soon to become unmanageable.

This colony is useful to the neighbourhood, a term which includes a large space here : it furnishes from its store many articles of great value, not so well supplied elsewhere ; and it is a market for all spare produce. There are also valuable culinary plants and fruit trees, for which the neighbourhood is indebted to the Harmonites ; and they set a good example of neatness and industry: but they are despised as ignorant ; and men are not apt to imitate what they scorn. Ignorant as the mass of Harmonites may be, when we contrast their neatness and order, with the slovenly habits of their neighbours, we see the good arising from mere *association*, which advances these poor people a century, probably much more, on the social scale, beyond the solitary beings who build their huts in the wilderness. For my reflections on the principles which may be supposed to actuate the rulers of this highly prosperous community, having no personal knowledge of the parties who govern, nor intimacy with any of the governed, I have no data, except the simple and, possibly, superficial observations of a traveller. Should I in this character have under-rated or mistaken them, I shall, when their neighbour, gladly repair my error.

From our entrance into the state of Ohio, at
Wheeling, to the southern boundary of the
Illinois, there is, properly speaking, no *capital*
employed in agriculture, as far as our observations extended.

The little that exists, over and above the
value of the soil, is to be seen in towns, in the
stores, and in mills.

The whole stock of the first settlers generally
consisted in their two hands; and the property
they now possess—the fruit of the labour of
these hands—can hardly be considered as capital employed in agriculture, as the sum of the
best improvements yet effected, only consists in
a few more of the *necessaries* of life ; and when
the little money that is obtained for produce is
expended in further improvements, the cultivator merely suspends his right to partake of
its *comforts.* He has no capital, properly speaking, employed in agriculture, whilst he remains
unfurnished with the means of comfortable
living.

As exceptions to the universal bareness and
poverty of the country in regard of capital,
there are a few instances in which its association with the physical power of numbers, has
produced effects so marvellous, that it seems to
be equally marvellous that such striking advan-

tages should not have produced more undertakings of a similar nature.

The instances I allude to, are the two settlements of the Shakers, one near Lebanon in the
state of Ohio, and the other on the Wabash,
fifteen miles north of Vincennes, in the state of
Indiana :—also the original establishment of
Mr. Rapp and his followers in Pennsylvania,
and their present wonderful colony of Harmony, on the Wabash, thirty miles south of
this place.

In the institution of these societies, the
Shakers and the Harmonites,—religion, or, if
you will, fanaticism, seems to be an agent so
powerful, and in fact *is* so powerful in its
operation on the conduct of their members, that
we are apt to attribute all the wonders that
arise within the influence of this principle to its
agency alone: for what may not be effected,
by a sentiment which can bear down and abrogate entirely, in the instance of the Shakers,
and nearly so in that of the Harmonites, the first
great and fundamental law of human, or rather
of *all*, nature? I allude to the tenet which is
avowed in the former, and more obscurely in-
culcated in the latter, that the gospel of Christ
is offered to them under the injunction of ab-
stinence from sexual intercourse.

I have had repeated opportunities of personal

observation, on the effects of the united efforts
of the Harmonites. The result of a similar
union of powers among the Shakers, has been
described to me by a faithful witness ; and I
am quite convinced that the association of numbers, in the application of a good capital, is
sufficient to account for all that has been done :
and that the unnatural restraint, which forms
so prominent and revolting a feature of these
institutions, is prospective, rather than immediate in its object.

It has, however, as I before remarked, the
mischievous tendency to render their example,
so excellent in other respects, altogether un-
availing. Strangers visit their establishments,
and retire from them full of admiration ; but, a
slavish acquiescence under a disgusting superstition, is so remarkable an ingredient in their
character, that it checks all desire of imitation.

I wish to see capital and population concen-
trated, with no bond of cohesion, but common
interest arising out of vicinity : the true elements, as I conceive, of a prosperous community.

The effects of this simple association would
not be so immediately striking as those above
mentioned, because the entire physical strength
of the society could not be directed to one
point, but would be apparent after a little time.
Such a society needs only room to prosper.

No emancipation or breaking up would be feared or thought of.

There is a plan before us, not yet sufficiently matured for publication, which I hope may, at no distant time, afford to some of our country-men the means of proving, that capital, skill, and industry, are capable of changing "a wilderness into a fruitful field," without the stimulus of fanaticism, or the restraints of superstition. The leading features of this scheme are, that men of capital who shall embark in it may, by affording to the poor the means of escaping from their sufferings, secure to themselves those enjoyments and habits of life to which their station in society has accustomed them; and obviating in respect to both classes the chief inconveniences of emigration.

The great want of capital in this country is evinced by this circumstance: the growers of "corn" (Indian corn) and other grain, sell at this season regularly, under the knowledge that it will as regularly advance to double the price before the next harvest. We now have an offer of two hundred barrels of "corn," five bushels to the barrel, at a dollar per barrel, when the seller is quite aware that it will be worth two dollars per barrel at Midsummer. Thus store-keepers, or other capitalists, receive as much for the crop, clear of expences, as the grower himself, who clears the land, ploughs, sows, and reaps it. We may judge from this consideration how much the farmer is kept back for want of spare capital; and what will be the advantages of the settler who commands it. The same remark applies to bacon, and every article of produce.

We must not suppose, that the poor farmer who is obliged to sell under such a disadvantage, is absolutely *poor*. He is, on the contrary, a thriving man. Probably, the person who now spares us from his heap, two hundred barrels of corn, possessed three years ago, nothing but his wife and family, his hands, and his title to a farm where an axe had never been lifted. He now, in addition, has a cabin, a barn, stable, horses, cows, and hogs; implements, furniture, grain, and other provision; thirty or forty acres of cleared land, and more in preparation, and well fenced; and his quarter section in its present state, worth four times its cost. He is growing rich, but he would proceed at a double speed, if he had the value of one year's crop beforehand : such is the general condition of new settlers.

A good cow and calf is worth from twelve to twenty dollars ; a two year old heifer, six dollars ; sheep are scarce ; ewes are worth about three dollars a head ; a sow three dollars ; a stout horse for drawing, sixty dollars or up-wards.

Wheat sells at 3s. 4½d. sterling, per bushel, Winchester measure.

Oats, 1s. 4d.

Indian corn, 11d.

Hay, about 35s. per ton.

Flour, per barrel, 36s.: 196 lb. nett.

Fowls, 4½d. each.

Eggs, ½d.

Butter, 6d. per pound.

Cheese, rarely seen, 13½d. per lb.

Meat, 2d. per lb.

A buck, 4s. 6d. without the skin.

Salt, 3s. 4d. per bushel.

Milk, given away.

Tobacco, 3d. per pound.

Our design was to commence housekeeping, but, being near the tavern, we continued to board there. This is more convenient to us, as there is but a poor market in this little town, and the tavern charges are reasonable. Our board is two dollars per week, each person, for which we receive twenty-one meals. Excellent coffee and tea, with broiled chickens, bacon, &c. for breakfast and supper; and variety of good but simple fare at dinner; about five-pence sterling a meal. No liquor but water is thought of at meals in this country, besides coffee, tea, or milk.

Travelling expences are very regular and moderate, amounting to a dollar per day, for man and horse,—viz.—

Breakfast and feed for horse ...... 37$\frac{1}{2}$ Cents
Feed for horses at noon.......... 12$\frac{1}{2}$
Supper, and lodging, man and horse 50

———

100 that is 1 dollar.

The power of capital in this newly settled or *settling* reigon, is not thoroughly understood in the eastern states, or emigration would not be confined to the indigent or laborious classes. These seem to be all in motion; for the tide sets far more strongly from these states towards the west, than from all Europe together. Trade follows of course; and it is not surprising that old America no longer affords a sure asylum for the distressed of other countries.

I am fully convinced, that those who are not screwed up to the full pitch of enterprize had better remain in old England, than attempt agriculture or business of any kind (manual operations excepted) in the Atlantic states. Emigrants from Europe are too apt to linger in the eastern cities, wasting their time, their money, and their resolution. They should push out

westward without delay, where they can live
cheaply until they fix themselves. Two dollars,
saved in Pennsylvania, will purchase an acre of
good land in the Illinois.

The land carriage from Philadelphia, to
Pittsburg, is from seven to ten dollars per cwt.
(100 lb.) Clothing, razors, pocket-knives, pen-
cils, mathematical instruments, and light articles in general, of constant usefulness, ought to
be carried even at this expence, and books,
which are scarce, and much wanted in the west.
Good gun-locks are rare and difficult to procure. No heavy implements will pay carriage.

A pocket compass is indispensable for every
stranger who ventures alone into the woods of
America ; and he should always carry the means
of lighting a fire : for the traveller, when he
starts in the morning on a wilderness journey,
little knows where next he may lay his head.—
Tow rubbed with gunpowder is good tinder :
—a few biscuits, a phial of spirits, a tomahawk,
and a good blanket, are necessary articles.
Overtaken by night, or bewildered, if thus provided, you may be really comfortable by your
blazing fire ; when without them, you would
feel dismal and disconsolate. A dog is a pleasant and useful fellow-traveller in the backwoods. You should make your fire with a fallen
tree for a back-log, and lie to leeward, with

your feet towards it. The smoke flying over, will preserve you from the damp air, and musquitoes. Tie your horse with a long rein, to the end of a bough, or the top of a young hickery tree, which will allow him to graze or browse; and change his position if you awake in the night.

Princeton, August 4. When the back country of America is mentioned in England, musquitoes by night, and rattlesnakes by day, never fail to alarm the imagination; to say nothing of wolves and bears, and panthers, and Indians still more ferocious. Our course of travelling from the mouth of James River, and over the mountains, up to Pittsburg, about five hundred miles; then three hundred miles through the woods of the state of Ohio, down to Cincinnati; next across the entire wilderness of Indiana, and to the extreme south of the Illinois:—This long and deliberate journey, one would suppose, might have introduced our party to an intimate acquaintance with some of these pests of America. We have, it is true, killed several of the serpent tribe; black snakes, garter snakes, &c.; and have *seen* one rattlesnake of extraordinary size. We have had musquitoes in a few damp spots, just as we should have had gnats in England. In our late expeditions in the Illinois, where we have led

the lives of thorough backwoods' men, if we
have been so unfortunate as to pitch our tent
on the edge of a creek, or near a swamp, and
have mismanaged our fire, we have been teazed
with musquitoes, as we might have been in the
fens of Cambridgeshire: this is the sum total
of our experience of these reported plagues.

But, for this forbearance, ample amends are
made by the innumerable tormentors which
assail you in almost every dwelling, till at
length you are glad, as evening approaches, to
avoid the abodes of man, and spread your pallet
under the trees.

This in-doors calamity is so universal in the
backwoods that it seems to be unavoidable, and
is submitted to as such with wondrous equani-
mity: by degrees, however, as the present
wretched and crowded hovels shall give place
to roomy and convenient habitations, the spirit
of cleanliness will gain admission, and the
miseries which always accompany filth and disorder will be brushed away, as the plagues of
Egypt were charmed by Aaron's rod.

Wolves and bears are extremely numerous,
and (especially the latter) very injurious to the
newly-settled districts. Hogs, which are a main
dependance for food as well as profit, are their
constant prey; and their holds are so strong,
that the hunters are unable to keep down their

numbers. There is a swamp of several miles in length, to the north of Shawnee Town, (and, I am told, there are many other such places) which is only passable for man over the dams made by beavers ; here the bears are absolute : the swamp affords abundance of food for hogs also, and they *will* resort to it. Yesterday, as I was riding along the side of this swamp, a farmer told me he had lost eight large hogs there this summer.

The wolves are very destructive to both hogs and sheep ; but they seldom attack sheep till a few years after a settlement has been made, when accident or hunger induces them to make trial of mutton ; and when they have once tasted it they are not easily deterred. Bears are lean in summer and very swift of foot, so that dogs can hardly overtake them ; but in winter they grow excessively fat on hickery nuts and other kinds of mast, and are unable to run for want of breath ; and this is the season of bear-hunting. The flesh of bears is in high estimation, and the skin is worth from three to five dollars, according to the size.—Neither of these marauders attack man unless when they are wounded, when they turn on the hunter with great fury.

August 5. The heat of this climate is not so oppressive to my feelings in the open prairies as in the deep woods, nor in either so much so as I expected. I have been using strong exercise through three of the hottest days that have been experienced for years, as say the people who talk of the weather, in the prairies—at Shawnee Town, on the Ohio, and here at Princeton— "How did you stand the heat of Sunday, Monday, and Tuesday?" The fact was, that, on one of those days, I walked with my gun in the prairie, exposed to the sun's rays, in quest of turkies, and travelled on horseback the other two, without great inconvenience. There is the comfort of a breeze every day; and the only breezeless sultry night I have experienced, proved the prelude to a thunder storm the succeeding day.

I think it may be attributed to these frequent thunder storms, that the summers of this climate are so pleasant and salubrious. When the fervency of the season becomes oppressive, suddenly the clouds collect, and a few rattling peals are heard; if near, accompanied by a soaking shower; if at a distance, you have no rain; but the cooling invigorating effect is soon perceived in the atmosphere.

August 7. We are now domiciliated in Princeton. Though at the farthest limits of Indiana, but two years old, and containing about fifty houses, this little town affords respectable society: it is the county-town, and can boast as many well-informed genteel people, in proportion to the number of inhabitants, as any county-town I am acquainted with. I think there are half as many individuals who are entitled to that distinction as there are houses, and not one decidedly vicious character, nor one that is not able and willing to maintain himself.

August 9. In my note of June 22, in which I attempted to give an outline of our views, regarding the settlement we were in quest of, is a remark on the increasing facility of accomplishing the upward navigation of the Mississipi and Ohio, by means of steam; from which it was inferred, that the grand intercourse between this western world, and Europe, would be through the Mississipi; and that consequently, the lower down the Ohio would eventually be the nigher to Europe.

We have, at length, dropped our anchor where we communicate with that river five hundred miles nearer to New Orleans than Cincinnati, where that note was written; and the following extract from the log book of the steam boat Etna, in the Louisville Courier, which we have just received, comes very seasonably in confirmation of that opinion: it is curious in itself, and a specimen of the local intelligence, which furnishes materials for our western journalists.

The average of speed against stream, of a steam-vessel heavily laden, is about sixty miles a-day. Their loading upwards, consists of dry goods, pottery, cotton, sugar, wines, liquors, salted fish, &c. besides passengers: downwards, of grain, flour, tobacco, bacon, &c. A considerable number of these vessels, I believe, about twenty-five, measuring from fifty to four hundred tons burthen, are now plying on these rivers; generally built at Pittsburg, or their machinery prepared there.

Extract from the Log Book of the Steam-Boat, Etna, de Hart, from New Orleans, to Louisville.

1817, June 6. Left New Orleans.
       12. Arrived at Natchez.--Left 15th.
       18. Passed the barge, Mary Ann, bound up above the gulph.
       19. Passed the barge, Cincinnati, above the Yazoo river.
       20. Passed the barge, General Washington, below the Crow's-nest.
       24. In the morning, below the Axkansas, met the Franklin.

1817, June 26.   Passed the steam-boat, Buffalo, Captain Sturges, bound up, thirty miles below the river St. Francis. At three P. M. met the steam-boat, Kentucky, seven days from the Falls.

28.   Passed the steam-boat, Harriet, above the Grand Cut-off, with a leaky boiler. One P. M. met the steam-boat, Washington, Captain Shrove, thirty miles below Chickesaw Bluffs, four days from the Falls. Four P. M. met the steam-boat, Vesuvius, de Hart, eighteen miles below the Bluffs; three days and a half from the Falls.

July 1.   Passed the barge Independance, fifty-five days, from New Orleans, above the Devil's Race Ground. Also passed a sloop barge.

6.   About New Madrid passed a sloop barge.

8.   In the Ohio, below the Three Sisters, passed the barge Expedition.

1817, July 10. Stopped and discharged **cargo**
at Shawnee Town.

11. Stopped and discharged cargo
at Henderson.

13. Passed the Triton Baum, in the
Mouth of Sinking Creek,
discharging cargo.

14. At four, A. M. passed a sloop
barge at Big Blue River.—
Arrived at Louisville.

On this voyage she passed, or met, five other
steam-boats, besides the Franklin and Triton,
which I suspect were also steam-boats. Nine-
tenths of the trade is yet carried on in the
usual craft; flat-boats, barges, piragues, &c.

Shawnee Town is 1,200 miles from New Orleans, which distance may be performed in
twenty days, provided there are no delays.
This is the nearest point on the Ohio to our
intended residence, (45 miles distance,) and
may therefore be considered as our shipping
port, from which we have navigable communication, by the Wabash, into our immediate
vicinity.

Thus situated, in the interior of a vast continent, we may have communication with Europe,
either for the export of produce or the introduction of merchandise, calculating on the addition of a month to the voyage across the Atlantic.

August 10. It is even so. See note of July 7. We are on the confines of society, among the true backwoods' men. We have been much among them—have lodged in their cabins, and partaken of their wretched and scanty fare : they have been our pilots to explore situations still more remote, and which only hunters visit.

From a nearer view of these people, something must be withdrawn from the picture which is given of their moral character, in the note above referred to.

It is rather an ill-chosen or unfortunate attachment to the hunters' life, than an unprincipled aversion to the regulations of society, which keeps them aloof from the abodes of more civilized men.

They *must* live where there is plenty of "bear and deer, and wild honey." Bear-hunting is their supreme delight: to enjoy this they are content to live in all manner of wretchedness and poverty : yet they are not savage in disposition, but honest and kind ; ready to forward our wishes, and even to labour for us, though our coming will compel them to remove to the "outside" again.

Not a settlement in this country is of a year's standing—no harvest has yet rewarded their toil ; but our approach, as I anticipated, will dislodge many of them, unless they should be tempted by our dollars to try the effect of labour, instead of the precarious supply derived from their beloved rifle. Half-a-dozen of these people, who had placed themselves round a beautiful prairie, have, in fact, come forward to sell us their all,—fat cattle, hogs, and this their first crop of corn, now just maturing: if we purchase they will go to some deeper recess, and build other cabins, and prepare cattle and corn, to be again quitted at the approach of some succeeding adventurers like ourselves; who may be considered, in this view, as the next grade in society.

But, that our friends in England, who may read these notes, may have an idea of our real position, let them consider our two families, viz. that of my friend Mr. George Flower, late of Marden, in England, and my own, about to be fixed upon eligible sites on our two adjoining estates, of fifteen hundred acres each, which we have carved for ourselves from a beautiful prairie and the adjoining woods.

Here we are preparing to raise buildings: carpenters and builders have offered themselves; estimates are made, and materials are at hand. We are also providing for gardens and orchards, that we may literally " sit under our own vines and our own fig trees." We might now mow many hundred acres of valuable grass if we had a good stock of cattle to require it.

The fee simple of each of these estates amounts to three thousand dollars, £675 sterling ; they are liable to a land tax of thirty dollars a-year to the general government, and about the same to the county, together something more than one penny per acre.

We shall have a certain and good market for produce from the growing population ; or by export down the Ohio.

Cattle and hogs thrive well, and even fatten, especially the latter, to a great size on the food they find ; and there is no bound to the number that may be raised, but in the ability of the breeder : they require little care, except to protect them from bears and wolves—keeping them tame, by giving them salt frequently.

On these estates we hope to live much as we have been accustomed to live in England : but this is not the country for fine gentlemen or fine ladies of any class or description, especially for those who love state, and require abundance of attendants.

To be easy and comfortable here, a man should know how to wait upon himself, and practise it, much more, indeed, than is common among the Americans themselves, on whom the accursed practice of slave-keeping has, I think, entailed habits of indolence, even where it has been abolished : it has also produced, among those who have no objection to earning their subsistence by labour in any other way, a bigotted aversion to domestic service. House-slaves are called " servants," and the word " slave" and servant," are in many places synonymous, meaning " slave." Thus abhorring the name of domestic service, as implying slavery, they keep their young people at home in indolence, and often in rags, when they might be improved in every way, by the easy employment offered them in the farms of their more affluent neighbours.

This prejudice against a name, I should think might gradually be surmounted by good management, and the powerful co-operation of self-interest. But however this may be, families, who remove into western America, either from Europe, or the Atlantic states, should bring with them the power and the inclination to dispense in a great degree, with domestic servants. How far this may be carried, consistently with real comfort, is yet to be proved ; but I believe, very far, by the aid of various mechanical and economical contrivances, which money may procure where it cannot procure servants ; and these aided by a simple system of living.

After all, some real convenience, and some agreeable reflections, arise out of the scarcity of domestics:—parade entertainments are discouraged by it ; and, if altogether relinquished, so much the better: hospitality need not suffer.

There is also compensation for some privations, in reflecting that you are not here surrounded by crowds of indigent fellow-creatures, who would gladly pick the crumbs that fall from your table: with more of these, the rich might better supply their domestic establishments: but who is the American who desires such a state of things?

The inconvenience sustained by a few may be cheerfully borne when we consider that it arises out of the general prosperity.

August 31. On revising these notes, I find some passages which will not suit the taste of such of my former or my present countrymen, (for I now consider myself an American) as have a relish for national flattery :—but as truth has been my sole object, I deserve their confidence ; and shall obtain it, though it may be with some degree of reluctance: and thus my end will be accomplished, which was to inform, rather than to please.

The world we have left at so remote a distance, and of which we hear so little, seems, to my imagination, like a past scene, and its transactions, as matter rather of history, than of present interest : but there are times, when the recollection of individuals, dear to us, and whom we cannot hope to meet again on earth, might be too painful ; but the occupations which surround us soon demand our attention, and afford,—not a cure—for this, which is the only serious ill which we experience from our change, but a sure alleviation.

The report of our intended establishment in the Illinois spreads far and wide ; and such is the attraction of population to capital, that many entries are already made by new settlers in our intended neighbourhood, and applications occur daily from many who are desirous of moving to us, as we may be in a condition to provide them with employment.

Our design is to commence operations by building a number of cabins with inclosures of two acres and a half each, along the sides of a section, which is to be reserved as their cow pasture.

These cottages, and inclosures, with a well between two, may be rented by persons who will resort to us for the sake of good earnings. If they were ready I think they would be occupied by handicraftsmen immediately; that is, as soon as the transport of their families could be effected.

The proposals, which have been already made, anticipating our views warrant this conclusion.

Here then, is a town about to rise before us ; of no equivocal origin, but the necessary result of capital applied to cultivation under these favourable circumstances.

I alluded, some pages back, to a larger plan, which we had in contemplation, not then sufficiently matured to be laid fully before our friends.

Since the writing of that note, our scheme has acquired so much consistency, that we think it safe to make some addition to that general sketch

It is the intention of my friend Mr. Flower, and myself, to purchase, on terms as favourable as can be obtained from the government, one, or more, entire townships in the Illinois territory, where the country is partly prairie, and partly woodland.

A township comprises thirty-six square miles, or sections of six hundred and forty acres each; in all, twenty-three thousand and forty acres.

These lands we propose to offer (on terms proportionably favourable) to a number of our countrymen, whose views may so far accord with our own, as to render proximity of settlement desirable.

In the sale of public lands, there is a regulation, which I have before mentioned, that the

sixteenth section, which is nearly the centre of
every township, shall not be sold. It is called
the reserved section; and is, accordingly, reserved for public uses in that township, for the
support of the poor, and for purposes of education.

This section, being of course, at the disposal
of the purchasers of the entire township, we
shall, by judicious arrangements, provide out of
it, not only for the objects which the wisdom of
the legislature had in view, but for the present
accommodation of the more indigent, but not
the least valued members of our proposed community. To obviate the sufferings to which
emigrants of this class are exposed on their
arrival, it is a material part of our plan to have
in readiness for every poor family, a cabin, an
inclosed garden, a cow, and a hog, with an
appropriation of land, for summer and winter
food for cows, proportioned to their number.

With regard to the disposal of the lands in
general, we shall probably offer them in sections,
half-sections, quarters, and eighths; that is, in
allotments of six hundred and forty, three hundred and twenty, one hundred and sixty, and
eighty acres, making other reservations of portions for public uses, as circumstances may
require.

We wish it to be clearly understood, that we

have no design of forming a society of English,
to be governed by any laws or regulations of our
own framing. We would not bind others, nor
be ourselves bound by any ties but those of
mutual interest, and good neighbourhood ; nor
be subject to any law, but the law of the land.

Yet, as concentration of capital, as well as of
population, will be essential to the rapid prosperity of our colony, we shall make a stipulation,
which we hope will be generally approved :—

That no person may be tempted, by the low
price at which our lands shall be offered to
possess themselves of it as a mere object of
speculation, a declaration will be required on
the part of the purchaser, of his intention to
reside on the spot.

We would, at the same time, impress upon
him the necessity of not purchasing more than
he can fairly manage.

Our opinion is, that it would be more advantageous to the resident proprietor to possess a
capital of four or five pounds sterling an acre,
than to incapacitate himself for carrying on his
improvements for want of adequate means.

I repeat, that we have not fallen on this
scheme from a wish to form a society exclu-
sively English, or, indeed, *any* society as distinct from the people at large. We would
most willingly extend our proposals to Ameri-

cans or emigrants of any nation, with the requisite capital, could our plan embrace them. Concentration of capital and numbers is the only refuge from many privations, and even sufferings in these remote regions:—but, the main advantage of preparing, as we propose, for the reception of our brethren, will be to save them a wearisome and expensive travel, in quest of a settlement, but too often ending in despair. Twelve long months spent in roaming over this wilderness, has broken the spirits, and drained the purses of many who would have done well, had they proceeded at once to a place provided:—also, to afford immediate protection and employment to *poor* emigrants.

Having proceeded thus far in the developement of our plan, it may materially forward its completion to take one step farther;—that is, to open a channel of communication with those who may be so well pleased with it, as to wish to join in its execution.

Such persons, if they cannot otherwise obtain satisfactory information, will please to direct their inquiries, to myself, at Princeton, Gibson County, Indiana.

THE END.

LETTERS FROM ILLINOIS

LETTERS

FROM

ILLINOIS.

BY MORRIS BIRKBECK,

AUTHOR OF " NOTES ON A TOUR THROUGH FRANCE," AND OF " NOTES ON
A JOURNEY IN AMERICA," &c.

" VOX CLAMANTIS È DESERTO."

THIRD EDITION.

LONDON:

PRINTED FOR TAYLOR AND HESSEY,
93, FLEET STREET.

1818.

LETTERS FROM ILLINOIS

First Edition 1818

Third Edition 1818

(London: *Printed for* Taylor & Hessey, *93 Fleet Street*, 1818)

PREFACE.

Most of these Letters were written to my intimate friends; others are in reply to applications made to me by entire strangers, for advice or information, some directing their inquiries to one point, and some to another. In answering, I generally kept pretty much to the tenor of the questions, as there would have been no end of the labour of communicating to every one, separately, information on every topic; yet, to some or other of my correspondents, I have had occasion to touch on most subjects interesting to an emigrant.

This consideration has induced me to publish the Letters, in the hope that, as a collection, they may be useful to others, as well as to the individuals to whom they were severally addressed.

It has been the fashion, though now a little out of date, for such as myself to be told that we were not fit to breathe the air of Old England; and, as we did not " like " the way of being ruled and taxed by people who had no more right to rule and tax us than consisted in the power of doing it, the land we lived in was too *good* for us, and it would be well for us to " leave it." At length things *improved* so much and so rapidly, that I began to think so too, and determined to try this country.

It is no more than due to those gentlemen and others, who were in the habit of recommending this little remedy of exile from the land of our fathers as a cure for our discontent, to inform them that, in my case, it has succeeded to admiration.

This should double their zeal. If they discover any of their neighbours weary and heavy laden, and therefore dissatisfied with our excellent constitution as now administered, let them earnestly recommend the same course to them which they recommended to me.

And by way of testimonial of its efficacy, I beg leave to offer the following Letters to the perusal of those gentlemen, and through them to their patients, who may thus, by the combined operations of leading and driving, be put in the way of obtaining speedy relief, and many a bad *subject* may become a good *citizen*.

There are, however, many of the restless whom this prescription would suit but badly. If low indulgence or unsated avarice have soured their tempers, it is not in

a transfer from the old establishments of
society to the silent waste where it scarcely
is begun, that they will find a cure. Envy
or disappointed ambition—have these dis-
gusted them with the world? The wilds
of Illinois will yield no repose to their per-
turbed spirits. The fiends will migrate
with them.

As little would I encourage the emigration of the tribe of grumblers, people who
are petulant and discontented under the
every-day evils of life. Life has its petty
miseries in all situations and climates, to
be mitigated or cured by the continual
efforts of an elastic spirit, or to be borne,
if incurable, with cheerful patience. But
the peevish emigrant is perpetually com-
paring the *comforts* he has quitted, but
never could enjoy, with the *privations* of his
new allotment. He overlooks the present
good, and broods over the evil with ha-

bitual perverseness; whilst in his recollection of the past he dwells on the good only.
Such people are always bad associates, but
they are an especial nuisance in an infant
colony.

CONTENTS.

LETTER I.

LETTER II.

LETTER VI.

LETTER VII.

LETTER VIII.

LETTER IX.

LETTER X.

LETTER XI.

LETTER XII.

LETTER XIII.

LETTER XIV.

LETTER XV.

LETTER XVI.

LETTER XXII.

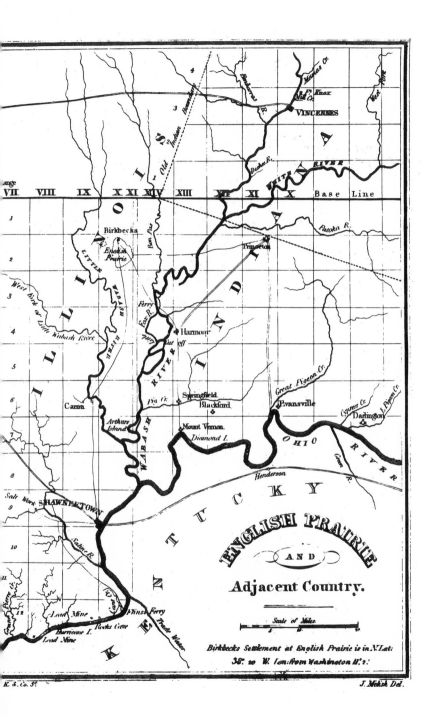

English Prairie and Adjacent Country.

Birkbecks Settlement at English Prairie is in N. Lat:
38° 20 W. lon: from Washington 11°.?.

L E T T E R S, &c.

LETTER I.

DEAR SIR,   *Nov.* 22, 1817.

I WROTE to you in June, soon after our entrance into the western territory; and now that I am settled down, having reached the point I aimed at on starting, and which seemed continually to recede as we advanced, I again take up my pen.

You and our other friends have probably wondered at our having proceeded so far west; and it would be difficult to make intelligible, to any but those who have seen this country, the motives which have constantly impelled as well as attracted us, as every step seems to you a further departure from home, and to be attended by additional privations.

This is in some degree true, as regards the first; but though the absolute distance is increased, the means of communication, by navigation to our neighbourhood, more than compensates; and in regard to the latter (as to additional privations), the case is far otherwise.

Had we remained in the state of Ohio, we must have paid from twenty to fifty dollars per acre for land which is technically called " improved," but is in fact deteriorated; or have purchased, at an advance of 1000 or 1500 per cent. unimproved land from speculators: and in either case should have laboured under the inconvenience of settling detached from society of our own choice, and without the advantage of choice as to soil or situation. We saw many eligible sites and fine tracts of country, but these were precisely the sites and the tracts which had secured the attachment of their possessors.

It was in fact impossible to obtain for ourselves a good position, and the neighbourhood of our friends, in the state of Ohio, at a price which common prudence would justify, or indeed at *any* price. Having given up the Ohio, we found nothing attractive on the eastern side of Indiana; and situations to the south, on the Ohio river bounding that state, were so well culled as to be in the predicament above described; offering no room

for us without great sacrifices of money and
society. The western side of Indiana, on the
banks of the Wabash, is liable to the same and
other objections. The northern part of Indiana is
still in possession of the Indians.

But a few miles farther west opened our way
into a country preferable in itself to any we had
seen, where we could choose for ourselves, and to
which we could invite our friends; and where, in
regard to communication with Europe, we could
command equal facilities, and foresee greater, than
in the state of Ohio, being so much nearer the
grand outlet at New Orleans.

I am so well satisfied with the election we
have made, that I have not for a moment felt a
disposition to recede; and much as I should lament that our English friends should stop short
of us, some amends even for that would be made
by the higher order of settlers, whom similar
motives bring constantly into our very track. Society we shall not want, I believe; and with the
fear of that want every other fear has vanished.
The comforts and luxuries of life we shall obtain
with ease and in abundance: pomp and state will
follow but too quickly.

I hope you will have seen Mr. ——— before
this reaches you. My writing to you at all, when
you have the advantage of personal communica-

tion with him, may seem impertinent. Since he
left us I have built a temporary dwelling on my
intended settlement, and have spent some time
there. This has made me better acquainted with
our situation; and as further knowledge confirms
and increases my favourable view of it, my communication may have its use. I would not per-
suade or invite any one to follow us, but I wish
my friends to know that my undertaking proceeds
to my entire content.

Mr. ——— is now writing a very just and interesting detail of particulars, as to the present
condition of agriculture and trade, in a letter to
his father, which I hope you will see. The power
of capital here is great almost beyond calculation:
the difficulty seems to be in the choice of objects,
out of the various ways of doubling and redoubling
it, which present themselves to the enterprizing.
These I do not much attend to; my line is land
and cultivation. My intended settlement is a
square of a mile and a half each way, containing
1440 acres. I made an estimate a few days ago
for my own government merely, of the amount
required for my establishment on this estate, on a
liberal plan, which I shall copy faithfully, without
altering an item. This will enable you to compare
the situation and prospects of a farmer in England
with those of a proprietor in Illinois, at the outset.

As to the annual profits here, I am not yet prepared with data for a very particular statement. The price of wheat may be reckoned at three shillings and fourpence sterling per bushel, and of beef and pork at twopence per pound. The land is fertile and easy of tillage; the wear of ploughshares almost nothing, as they require sharpening by the smith but once a year; and we shall have labourers in plenty at a price not much exceeding that of England: putting horse labour and man's labour together, they will be quite as cheap. Then we have no rent, tithe, or poor's rate, and scarcely any taxes, perhaps one farthing per acre.

But omitting the annual income, about which I know enough to feel no anxiety, let us consider that at the end of fourteen years, when we may suppose the lease of the most favoured English farmers to terminate, a stock of various kinds, of great value, will be accumulated by the proprietor here; the worth of his estate, in the regular course of improvement, will be increased to the amount of 6 or 8,000*l.* and no *renewal* wanted; also, that the capital required by the English farmer of such an estate, is at least double to that required by the Illinois proprietor at the outset of the undertaking.

Copy from my Memorandum-Book.

Estimate of money required for the comfortable establishment of my family on Bolting-house, now English,
prairie; on which the first instalment is paid. About
720 acres of wood-land, and 720 prairie—the latter to
be chiefly grass :

Dollars.

Second instalment, August 1819, 720 dollars;
    Third, Aug. 1820, 720 dollars; Fourth, Aug.
    1821, 720 dollars 2,160

Dwelling-house and appurtenances   .   . 4,500

Other buildings .   .   .   .   · 1,500

4,680 rods of fencing; *viz.* 3,400 on the prairie,
    and 1,280 round the wood-land   .   . 1,170

Sundry wells, 200 dollars; gates, 100 dollars;
    cabins, 200 dollars   500

100 head of cattle, 900 dollars; 20 sows, &c. 100
    dollars; sheep, 1,000 dollars   .   . 2,000

Ploughs, waggons, &c. and sundry tools and im-
    plements   270

Housekeeping until the land supplies us   . 1,000

Shepherd one year's wages, herdsman one year,
    and sundry other labourers .   .   . 1,000

One cabinet-maker, and one wheelwright, one
    year, making furniture and implements, 300
    dollars each   600

Sundry articles of furniture, ironmongery, pottery,
    glass, &c.   500

Sundries, fruit-trees, &c.   .   .   .   100

                                      15,300

Dollars.

Brought forward . .	15,300
First instalment already paid . . .	720
Five horses on hand, worth . . .	300
Expense of freight and carriage of linen, bedding, books, clothing, &c. &c. . .	1,000
Value of articles brought from England . .	4,500
Voyage and journey	2,000

Dollars 23,820

£ 5,359 Sterling.

Allow about 600 dollars more for seed and corn	141

£ 5,500

I make no comment on the above: it would be best to talk it over together. I hope to hear from you at least, and remain sincerely yours.

LETTER II.

DEAR SIR,   *Nov.* 24, 1817.

I HAVE now been an inhabitant of this place more than four months; my plans of future life have acquired some consistency; I have chosen a situation, purchased an estate, determined on the position of my house, and have, in short, become so familiar with the circumstances in which I have thus deliberately placed myself and my family, that I feel qualified to give you a cool account of my experiences, — of the effect of this great change of condition on my mind, now that I may be supposed but little under the influence of the charm of novelty, or the stimulus of pursuit.

Whilst I had the company of Mr. ———, who, I hope, is at this moment your welcome guest, it might be well supposed that similarity of object and mutual consultation, by dividing would diminish my anxiety as to the event of our speculation. He left us on the sixth of September; and such is the uncertainty of all human affairs when *time* only is interposed between us and our intentions, that when in addition to time the *distance* of 5000 miles twice passed, was to intervene between our parting and re-union, I confess I have been apt to consider his return to our settlement in the light rather of a remote contingency, than as an event to be calculated on.

Thus, on his departure, we naturally fell back on our own resources. " Well, Sir," you will say, " and how did they sustain you?" I have not for a moment felt despondency, scarcely discouragement, in this happy country, this land of hope! Life

here is only *too* valuable, from the wonderful efficiency of every well-directed effort.   Such is the
field of delightful action lying before me, that I
am ready to regret the years wasted in the support
of taxes and pauperism, and to grieve that I am
growing old now that a really useful career seems
just beginning.   I am happier, much happier, in
my prospects : I feel that I am doing well for my
family; and the privations I anticipated seem to
vanish before us.

We shall have some English friends next summer; and a welcome they shall experience.   But
if not one had the resolution to follow the track
we have smoothed before them, we should never
wish to retrace it, except perhaps as travellers. As
to what are called the comforts of life, I feel that
they are much more easily attainable here than
they have ever been to me; and for those who
are to succeed me, I look forward with a pleasure
which can only be understood by one who has felt
the anxieties of an English father.

I expect to see around me in prosperity many
of my old neighbours, whose hard fare has often
embittered my own enjoyments.   Three of them
have already made the effort, and succeeded in
getting out to us.   This delights us, but we have
by no means depended on it; joyful as we are at
the prospect of giving them an asylum.

Two more are waiting at Philadelphia for an invitation which is now on its way. They wept at parting with their companions who are now here, but they wanted faith, thinking they would never reach our abode " *so far west*." And should faith be wanting to all whom we so earnestly wish to see, I believe not one of us would regret the step we have taken.

I have transmitted to Congress a memorial soliciting a grant, by way of purchase, of a tract of land. If it succeeds I shall be glad, because I think it may afford hundreds of families the relief we are now enjoying; but it does not promise much particular advantage to us, for I am well satisfied with our choice of situation; and this might retard our settlement, or render it proper to transfer ourselves to the proposed purchase. On a more deliberate view of the land we have selected, I am a little reluctant at the thought of being diverted from our first plan; and at all events, I would secure a good extent in our own neighbourhood.

I am, &c. &c.

P. S. If it were really so unwise to migrate westward, out of the tens (I was going to say hundreds) of thousands who move annually from the eastern states into this western wilderness, we

should hear of *some returning*. Mr. —— informs
me that he has given you a true account of things,
and told you what you are to expect. He knows
as much about the matter as you do about the
wilds of Siberia. 'Tis but a little time since a
horse that had travelled through Kentucky was
a sight in Philadelphia: and Kentucky is an old
country.

I have just read a statement of five hundred
emigrants per week passing through Albany westward, counting from the first of September. This
occurred on *one* road, and that far to the north.

I sat down to write to you under an impression
that you would be deterred, and might be prevented
from following us, by difficulties, some real and
serious, others not so; and I thought it might be
useful to you, as I knew it would be pleasant, to
find that I am satisfied as to my own undertaking.
It is for this reason that you are treated with so
much about myself. I wish I could put you in
possession of *all* my mind, my entire sentiments,
my daily and hourly feeling of contentment: not
that *you* would be warranted thereby to place yourself and family along-side of mine. You might,
however, from your knowledge of me and my
habits, which remain much the same, proceed in
your own estimate to some length.

LETTER III.

SIR,   *Nov.* 29, 1817.

IT would give me much pleasure to afford you satisfactory information on the several particulars you mention, but I am, like yourself, a stranger in this country, and can therefore only communicate to you my opinions in answer to your inquiries.

To the first, as to the most eligible part of the United States for obtaining improved *farms*, or uncultivated lands for Englishmen, &c. I reply, that with a view to the settlement of the number of families you mention, it will be vain to look for improved farms in any part that I have seen or heard of. Probably a single family might be suited in almost any large district, as the changes which are continually occurring in human affairs, will occasionally throw eligible farms into the market every where. But you can have no *choice* of cultivated lands, as those you would prefer are the least likely to be disposed of; and it is altogether unlikely you should meet with a body of such lands, for the accommodation of thirty or forty families; considering too, that, by travelling a few days' journey farther west, you may have a *choice* of land of equal value at one-tenth of the price, where they may settle contiguous, or at least near to each other. I have no hesitation in recommending you to do as I have done; that is, to head the tide of emigration, and provide for your friends where the lands are yet unappropriated.

After traversing the states of Ohio and Indiana, looking out for a tract suited to my own views, and those of a number of our countrymen who have signified their intentions of following our example, I have fixed on this spot in Illinois, and am the better pleased with it the more I see of it.

As to obtaining *labourers*. A single settler may get his labour done by the piece on moderate terms, not higher than in some parts of England; but if many families settle together, all requiring this article, and none supplying it, they must obtain it from elsewhere. Let them import English labourers, or make advantageous proposals to such as are continually arriving at the eastern ports.

Provisions are cheap of course. Wheat three and fourpence sterling per bushel. Beef and pork twopence per pound, groceries and clothing dear, building moderate, either by wood or brick. Bricks are laid by the thousand, at eight dollars or under, including lime.

Privations I cannot enumerate. Their amount depends on the previous habits and present disposition of individuals: for myself and family, the privations already experienced, or anticipated, are of small account compared with the advantages.

Horses, 60 to 100 dollars, or upwards; cows, 10 to 20 dollars; sows, 3 to 5 dollars.

Society is made up of new comers chiefly, and of course must partake of the leading characters of these. There is generally a little bias of attraction in a newly settled neighbourhood, which brings emigrants from some particular state or country to that spot; and thus a tone is given to the society. Where we are settling, society is yet unborn as it were. It will, as in other places, be made up of such as come; among whom English farmers, I presume, will form a large proportion.

Roads as yet are in a state of nature.

Purchases of land are best made at the land-offices: payments, five years, or prompt; if the latter, eight per cent. discount.

Mechanics' wages, 1 dollar to $1\frac{1}{2}$. Carpenters, smiths, shoemakers, brickmakers, and bricklayers, are among the first in requisition for a new settlement: others follow in course;—tanners, saddlers, tailors, hatters, tin-workers, &c. &c.

We rely on good *markets* for produce, through the grand navigable communication we enjoy with the ocean.

Medical aid is not of difficult attainment. The English of both sexes, and strangers in general, are liable to some bilious attacks on their first arrival: these complaints seem, however, simple, and not difficult to manage if taken in time.

The *manufactures* you mention may hereafter be eligible; cotton, woollen, linen, stockings, &c. Certainly not at present.   Beer, spirits, pottery, tanning, are objects of immediate attention.

The *minerals* of our district are not much known. We have excellent limestone; I believe we have coal: wood will, however, be the cheapest fuel for some years.

Implements are cheap till you commence with the iron. A waggon, 35 or 40 dollars, exclusive of tier to wheels. A strong waggon for the road complete will amount to 160 dollars or upwards.

The best *mode of coming* from England to this part of the western country is by an eastern port, thence to Pittsburg, and down the Ohio to Shaw-nee-town.   Clothing, bedding, household linen, simple medicines of the best quality, and sundry small articles of cutlery and light tools, are the best things for an emigrant to bring out.

I can hardly reply to your inquiry about the *manner of travelling;* it must be suited to the party.   Horseback is the most pleasant and expeditious; on foot the cheapest: a light waggon is eligible in some cases; in others the stage is a necessary evil.   I see I shall render you liable to

double postage, but I wished to reply to each of
your inquiries as far as I could.

To serve you or your friends will be a pleasure
to, Sir,

Yours, &c. &c.

———

LETTER IV.

DEAR SIR,   *Nov.* 30, 1817.

No doubt my son will have told you
what he has learnt of our proceedings from our
departure until our arrival here.   By April next I
hope we shall be fixed in our cabins on the prairie ;
and, in two years, I hope to see a populous and
thriving neighbourhood, where in July last I could
not find a single inhabitant.

As we travelled along, viewing the country,
and anxiously seeking a place of rest, I took short
notes of occurrences and observations ; and having
added an account of our intended settlement, with
a sketch of our plans and prospects, I sent it to the
press.   I directed a copy to be delivered to you,
which you probably will have received before this
reaches you. Having described things just as they
appeared to me, I am in hopes my friends will

collect from it a pretty clear idea of the state of
this remote country.

Beginning where that leaves off, you will suppose me busy enough in planning and preparing
for our new farm. I have secured a considerable
tract of land, more than I have any intention of
holding, that I may be able to accommodate some
of our English friends. Our soil appears to be
rich, a fine black mould, inclining to sand, from
one to three or four feet deep, lying on sandstone
or clayey loam; so easy of tillage as to reduce the
expense of cultivation below that of the land I
have been accustomed to in England, notwithstanding the high rates of human labour. The
wear of plough-irons is so trifling, that it is a
thing of course to sharpen them in the spring
once for the whole year. Our main object will be
live stock, cattle, and hogs, for which there is a
sure market at a good profit. Twopence a pound
you will think too low a price to include a profit;
but remember, we are not called upon, after receiving our money for produce, to refund a portion of it for rent, another portion for tithe, a
third for poor's rates, and a fourth for taxes; which
latter are here so light as scarcely to be brought
into the nicest calculation. You will consider also,
that money goes a great deal farther here, so that
a less profit would suffice. The fact is, however,

that the profits on capital employed any way in this country are marvellous: in the case of live-stock the outgoings are so small, that the receipts are nearly all clear.

The idea of exhausting the soil by cropping, so as to render manure necessary, has not yet entered into the estimates of the western cultivator. Manure has been often known to accumulate until the farmers have removed their yards and buildings out of the way of the nuisance. They have no notion of making a return to the land, and as yet there seems no bounds to its fertility.

For about half the capital that is required for the mere cultivation of our worn-out soils in England, a man may establish himself as a proprietor here, with every comfort belonging to a plain and reasonable mode of living, and with a certainty of establishing his children as well or better than himself—such an approach to certainty at least as would render *anxiety* on that score un-pardonable.

Land being obtained so easily, I had a fancy to occupy here just as many acres as I did at Wanborough; and I have added 160 of timbered land to the 1,440 I at first concluded to farm. I shall build and furnish as good a house as the one I left, with suitable outbuildings, garden, orchard, &c. make 5,000 rods of fence, chiefly bank

and ditch, provide implements, build a mill, support the expenses of housekeeping and labour until
we obtain returns, and pay the entire purchase-
money of the estate, for less than half the capital
employed on Wanborough farm. At the end of
fourteen years, instead of an expiring lease, I or
my heirs will probably see an increase in the value
of the land equal to fifteen or twenty times the
original purchase.

In the interval my family will have lived handsomely on the produce, and have plenty to spare,
should any of them require a separate establishment on farms of their own.

Thus I see no obstruction to my realising all
I wished for on taking leave of Old England. To
me, whose circumstances were comparatively easy,
the change is highly advantageous; but to labouring people, to mechanics, to people in general who
are in difficulties, this country affords so many
sure roads to independence and comfort, that it is
lamentable that any, who have the means of
making their escape, should be prevented by the
misrepresentation of others, or their own timidity.

You will gather from this letter, that the pre-
dictions of some of my old neighbours, who said
I should be soon glad to return to Wanborough,
are not in the way of being fulfilled. Some who
do not know me so well as you do, will perhaps

now doubt my sincerity. It would be no alleviation of my own troubles to lead others into the like; so that if I were disappointed, and had not the manliness to acknowledge it, I should at least hold my tongue.

My son never fails to mention, in his letters, his obligations to you for your truly kind notice of him in his fatherless condition. You find a reward for this in your own kind heart. Wishing you and yours all prosperity,

I remain, dear Sir,

sincerely yours.

LETTER V.

MY DEAR FRIEND,   *Dec.* 9, 1817.

. . . . And you would, I am certain, give me your congratulations, *almost* unmixed, had you a complete view of our comfortable situation and our prospects.

I enjoy the exchange more than you can conceive—much more than I ever anticipated; but not exactly with feelings such as you, partly in raillery and partly in seriousness, suppose, either with regard to the country I have quitted, and which I shall never cease to love, or with regard to the position I am to assume among my American brethren.

In England we find great simplicity, or rather ignorance, in the remote and little frequented districts : the inhabitants of the villages are for the most part the children of the former inhabitants, to be succeeded by their children, ploughing the same fields, and threshing in the same barns, from generation to generation. But we in this new country are a motley assemblage of adventurers; not one that is grown to man's estate was born in it. Coming hither mature in age and experience, we bring and throw into a common stock the knowledge of distant countries, and various climates ; and, when collected, a people of emigrants is the last to which we would apply the epithet of " *simple*," or of ignorant.

Thus I am in no danger of setting up for an arrogant instructor of " the simple Americans :" and yet the value of the little I know, and the little I can do beyond the reach of the mere husbandman, is greatly enhanced by transplantation. I believe you cannot have an adequate notion of the enlargement of the sphere of useful exertion which I experience ; and I utterly despair, *at present*, of convincing you that this most delightful acquisition costs so little as it does, in what are deemed, and properly, the enjoyments of social life. " Ah," say you, " happy enthusiast, his dream is not yet over."—There is, however, something real in the change from anxiety about the future to perfect tranquillity, and from a life of irksome toil to one of pleasurable exertion. There is a difference betwixt hope and fear that is not to be despised, even in *dreaming*. This is indeed a land of liberty and hope, and I rejoice unfeignedly that I am in it. Yet England was never so dear to me as it is now in the recollection: being no longer under the base dominion of her oligarchy, I can think of my native country, and her noble institutions, apart from her politics.

I read in the Philadelphia papers, of which I receive half a dozen per week, marvellous things from England, about gold and the funds; and melancholy accounts of the typhus fever in Ireland, and lately in Birmingham and Manchester, and even in London: how stands the case? I am apt to fear the misery is real, and the prosperity fallacious. . . . .

I am, &c. &c.

LETTER VI.

MY DEAR FRIEND, *Dec. 25, 1817.*

THERE are some truly estimable people here, of gentle manners, warm hearts, and cultivated understandings, to whom we are growing much attached. The decision of character which prevails among the new settlers renders their society very interesting; and there is a spirit of fearless enterprise which raises even the vicious above contempt. Not a family, hardly an individual, whose adventures would not highly amuse and astonish the groups assembled round the firesides of our old country at this story-telling season.

But what think you of a community, not only without an established religion, but of whom a large proportion profess no particular religion, and think as little about the machinery of it, as you know was the case with myself? What in some places is esteemed a decent conformity with practices which we despise, is here altogether unnecessary. There are, however, some sectaries even here, with more of enthusiasm than good temper; but their zeal finds sufficient vent in loud preaching and praying. The Court-house is used by all persuasions, indifferently, as a place of worship; any

acknowledged preacher who announces himself
for a Sunday or other day, may always collect an
audience, and rave or reason as he sees meet.
When the weather is favourable, few Sundays pass
without something of the sort. It is remarkable
that they generally deliver themselves with that
chaunting cadence you have heard among the
quakers. This is Christmas day, and seems to be
kept as a pure holiday—merely a day of relaxation
and amusement: those that choose, observe it
religiously ; but the public opinion does not lean
that way, and the law is silent on the subject.
After this *deplorable* account, you will not wonder
when you hear of earthquakes and tornados
amongst us. But the state of political feeling is,
if possible, still more deplorable. Republican
principles prevail universally. Those few zealous
persons, who, like the ten faithful that were *not*
found by Abraham, might have stood between
their heathen neighbours and destruction, even
these are among the most decided foes of all
legitimacy, except that of a government appointed
by the people. They are as fully armed with car-
nal weapons as with spiritual; and as determined
in their animosity against royalty and its appurtenances, as they are against the kingdom of Anti-
Christ; holding it as lawful to use the sword of
the flesh for the destruction of the one, as that of
the spirit for the other.

Children are not baptized or subjected to any superstitious rite; the parents name them, and that is all: and the last act of the drama is as simple as the first.   There is no consecrated burial place, or funeral service.   The body is enclosed in the plainest coffin; the family of the deceased convey the corpse into the woods; some of the party are provided with axes, and some with spades; a grave is prepared, and the body quietly placed in it; then trees are felled, and laid over the grave to protect it from wild beasts.   If the party belong to a religious community, preaching sometimes follows; if not, a few natural tears are shed in silence, and the scene is closed.   These simple monuments of mortality are not unfrequent in the woods.   Marriages are as little concerned with superstitious observances as funerals: but they are observed as occasions of festivity.   We are not quite out of hearing of the world and its bustle, but the sound is rather long in reaching us.   We receive the Philadelphia daily papers once a week, about a month after they are published; in these we read extracts from the English journals of the month preceding: so we take up the news as you forget it; and what happened three months ago in Europe is just now on the carpet here.

As to society, comparisons are odious; but, in good faith, I think you would have nothing to

regret in exchanging such a circle as I fancy yours
to be, for any circle that would surround you in
the inhabited part of these wild woods.

I am, my dear friend,

ever yours.

LETTER VII.

DEAR SIR,   *Jan.* 7, 1818.

I AM not so sanguine as yourself about
our old and once glorious England: such a ra-
tional, honest, economical system, as a true par-
liament would produce, might, twenty-six years
ago, have done something for us. Economy and
order are good to prevent ruin, but when all is
spent they are of small avail: besides, who *wishes*
for the experiment to be made? Not the fund-
holders, nor the borough-holders, nor the army—
a few, a very few political characters, and the
distressed of all classes. The latter, you will say,
are a formidable number. So they are; but they
are weak, and have nothing in common but their
misery. The " friends of order," that is, the bulk

of the people, who have as yet escaped pauperism, but are shivering on the brink, and fearful that the slightest change will plunge them into the gulf—these are the enemies of reform, and all the timid of every class.

Had I been an owner of land, I might possibly have staid by my paternal acres; or if I had been a single man (that is, a childless man), I might have remained in the hope of contributing to the work of reformation, or, in pure hatred of tyranny, to stand the brunt. But as I am circumstanced, I thought it right to withdraw, with my family, out of its reach; and I have not repented a single moment; on the contrary, I have every reason to rejoice in the change, for it is from gloom and despondency to tranquillity and hope.

As to the comforts and accommodations of life, we have our books, our music, our agreeable and kind neighbours, good food and clothing, and before two years are ended we expect to have as good and well-furnished a house as that we left. It is astonishing how small are the privations we are subject to. I counted the cost beforehand, but over-reckoned it; and we are of course the better satisfied.

It will be very long before travelling will be pleasant, except in fine weather and on horseback: this is the grand inconvenience of a new country;

but it is not to be compared to the inconvenience
of living at the mercy of a villainous aristocracy.
Why, Sir! I must either have sneaked about, in
what you call my country, a prisoner at large, or
amused myself with counting the nails on the
door of my dungeon. And so must you; for
things will not mend without a dreadful crisis:
and until that liberates you, you will be free only
by sufferance, " within the Rules."

Here, I shall be employed in enlarging the
circle of our enjoyments; there, I was contracting
it daily. My family had already made several
downward movements; we had learnt to dispense
with the comfort of a carriage; we mounted our
horses instead: this was no bad exchange; but
the cause of our making the exchange was irksome. From horseback, my daughters cheerfully
enough betook themselves to their feet: no great
harm in that, only it was by compulsion. So we
went down step by step.

Our friend Cobbett declaims about patriotism
in sounding phrases, but I adhere to the maxim
" ubi libertas ibi patria." What *is* country? the
soil? Of this I was only an occupant. The government? I abhorred its deeds and its principles.
The church? I did not believe in its doctrines,
and had no reverence for the clergy. The army?
No. The law? We have the same law here,

with some omissions and some improvements. The people? Yes; but not the fund-holders, nor the soi-disant House of Commons; not the consumers, nor the creators of taxes. My family and friends I love wherever I meet them: I have almost as many, and as strong ties of that sort, on this as on the other side of the Atlantic—soon I hope to have more, and then this will be my country.

I *own* here a far better estate than I *rented* in England, and am already more attached to the *soil*. Here, every citizen, whether by birthright or adoption, is part of the government, identified with it, not *virtually*, but in fact; and eligible to every office, with one exception, regarding the Presidency, for which a birthright is necessary.

I love this government; and thus a novel sensation is excited: it is like the developement of a new faculty. I am become a patriot in my old age: thus a new virtue will spring up in my bosom.

I am, &c.

LETTER VIII.

MY DEAR SIR,   *Jan.* 17, 1818.

I WROTE to you early in September, since
which I hope you have received a copy of my
journal. Thus having made you of our party on
the journey, and introduced you to some acquaintance with our Princeton affairs, I am now going
to take you to the prairies, to shew you the
very beginning of our settlement. Having fixed
on the north-western portion of our prairie for our
future residence and farm, the first act was building a cabin, about two hundred yards from the
spot where the house is to stand. This cabin is
built of round straight logs, about a foot in diameter, lying upon each other, and notched in at the
corners, forming a room eighteen feet long by sixteen; the intervals between the logs " chuncked,"
that is, filled in with slips of wood; and " mudded,"
that is, daubed with a plaister of mud: a spacious
chimney, built also of logs, stands like a bastion
at one end: the roof is well covered with four
hundred " clap boards" of cleft oak, very much
like the pales used in England for fencing parks.
A hole is cut through the side, called, very properly, the " door, (the through,)" for which there

is a " shutter," made also of cleft oak, and hung
on wooden hinges. All this has been executed by
contract, and well executed, for twenty dollars.   I
have since added ten dollars to the cost, for the
luxury of a floor and ceiling of sawn boards, and
it is now a comfortable habitation.

To this cabin you must accompany me, a
young English friend, and my boy Gillard, whom
you may recollect at Wanborough. We arrived
in the evening, our horses heavily laden with our
guns, and provisions, and cooking utensils, and
blankets, not forgetting the all-important axe. This
was immediately put in requisition, and we soon
kindled a famous fire, before which we spread our
pallets, and, after a hearty supper, soon forgot that
besides ourselves, our horses and our dogs, the
wild animals of the forest were the only inhabitants of our wide domain. Our cabin stands at
the edge of the prairie, just within the wood, so
as to be concealed from the view until you are at
the very door. Thirty paces to the east the prospect opens from a commanding eminence over the
prairie, which extends four miles to the south and
south-east, and over the woods beyond to a great
distance; whilst the high timber behind, and on
each side, to the west, north, and east, forms a
sheltered cove about five hundred yards in width.
It is about the middle of this cove, two hundred

and fifty yards from the wood each way, but open to the south, that we propose building our house.

Well, having thus established myself as a resident proprietor, in the morning my boy and I (our friend having left us) sallied forth in quest of neighbours, having heard of two new settlements at no great distance. Our first visit was to Mr. Emberson, who had just established himself in a cabin similar to our own, at the edge of a small prairie two miles north-west of us. We found him a respectable young man, more farmer than hunter, surrounded by a numerous family, and making the most of a rainy day by mending the shoes of his household. We then proceeded to Mr. Woodland's, about the same distance south-west: he is an inhabitant of longer standing, for he arrived in April, Mr. E. in August. He has since built for us a second cabin, connected with the first by a covered roof or porch, which is very convenient, forming together a commodious dwelling.

In our walk we saw no game but partridges, and a squirrel. We found plenty of grapes, which I thought delicious. The soil seemed to improve in fertility on closer inspection, and the country appeared more pleasant: in fact, my mind was at ease, and this spreads a charm over external objects.   Our township is a square of six miles each side, or thirty-six square miles; and what may properly be called our neighbourhood, extends about six miles round this township in every direction.   Six miles to the north is the boundary of surveyed lands.   Six miles to the east is the Bonpas, a stream which joins the Big Wabash about six miles south of us, where the latter river makes a bold bend to the west, approaching within six miles of the Little Wabash: this river forms our western boundary, at about the same distance up to the northern line of survey above-mentioned. The centre of this tract is our prairie, containing about 4,000 acres.

There are many other prairies, or natural meadows, of various dimensions and qualities, scattered over this surface, which consists of about two hundred square miles, containing perhaps twelve human habitations, all erected, I believe, within one year of our first visit—most of them within three months.   At or near the mouth of the Bonpas, where it falls into the Big Wabash, we project a shipping port: a ridge of high land, without any intervening creek, will afford an easy communication with the river at that place.

The Wabash, as you know, is a noble stream, navigable several hundred miles from its junction with the Ohio, and receiving other navigable rivers

in its course: White River in particular, opening a
communication with the most fertile region of
Indiana, will at a future day hold a distinguished
rank among rivers.   The country above, both on
the Wabash and White River, is peopling rapidly;
and there is, through the Ohio, a great natural
channel of intercourse between this vast country
and the ocean.   Steam-boats already navigate the
Wabash: a vessel of that description has this
winter made its way up from New Orleans to
within a few miles of our settlement.   They are
about building one at Harmony, twenty miles below, as a regular trader, to carry off the surplus
produce, and bring back coffee, sugar, and other
groceries, as well as European manufactures.

There are no very good mill-seats on the
streams in our neighbourhood, but our prairie,
affords a most eligible site for a windmill; we are
therefore going to erect one immediately: the
materials are in great forwardness, and we hope
to have it in order to grind the fruits of the ensuing harvest.

Two brothers, and the wife of one of them,
started from the village of Puttenham, close to
our old Wanborough, and have made their way
out to us: they are carpenters, and are now very
usefully employed in preparing the scantlings for
the mill, and other purposes.   You may suppose

how cordially we received these good people. They landed at Philadelphia, not knowing where on this vast continent they should find us : from thence they were directed to Pittsburg, a wearisome journey over the mountains of more than 300 miles ; at Pittsburgh they bought a little boat for six or seven dollars, and came gently down the Ohio, 1,200 miles, to Shawnee-town ; from thence they proceeded on foot till they found us. On their way they had many flattering offers ; but true to their purpose, though uninvited and unlooked for, they held out to the end, and I believe they are well satisfied with their reception and prospects.

By the first of March I hope to have two ploughs at work, and may possibly put in 100 acres of corn this spring. Early in May, I think, we shall be all settled in a convenient temporary dwelling, formed of a range of cabins of ten rooms, until we can accomplish our purpose of building a more substantial house. My young folks desire to be most kindly remembered to you : they are full of life and spirits ; not one of them, I believe, having felt a symptom of repentance from the commencement of our undertaking.

I remain, dear Sir,

ever yours.

LETTER IX.

DEAR SIR,

. . . . Money will go surprisingly
far in this country, yet capital is as necessary to
the full here as in England; indeed more so, because few persons have money to lend. Legal
interest is 6 per cent. but it is worth 12½ per cent.
to put in trade; and somehow or other this, like
other articles, finds its value in spite of the *maxi-
mum* established by law.

Efforts are now making in some parts of the
union, particularly in Virginia and North Carolina,
to do away the restraints on usury, which operate
merely as a tax on the needy borrower: should
this liberal principle succeed here, I think it will
be generally adopted; and will afford a new instance of the plain Americans doing right, whilst
the philosophers of Europe are reasoning about
it. . . . .

All the letters we have yet received from
England, were written before our friends had
heard of our establishment here, and we are becoming very anxious to know what you now think
of us, when our pilgrim state no longer calls for
your sympathy. The most zealous approvers of

the enterprise felt, I dare say, some little diffidence about it—some small misgivings as to our final success; but these will receive our professions of satisfaction cordially and with entire credence: others, still hesitating, will fancy they discover in all our accounts symptoms of latent discontent, concealed possibly from ourselves for the present, by our anxiety to make the best of things as we find them: others again, more positive of course in proportion as they recede from the truth, will see in our favourable reports of the country, its institutions, and people, a design to mislead, as we have been misled; or, overlooking those favourable views, they will dwell on the dark shades of the description, and rise from our account of America with a fresh stock of prejudice. Thus we are apt to speculate on your opinions about our proceedings; and you, the while, are probably too fully occupied with your own affairs to spare much attention to us and ours.

Winter is here, on the whole, an agreeable season; we have many days, and even weeks, which are truly delightful. Extreme cold does not seem to *belong* to us; but we have some very severe paroxysms of it when the wind sets in from the north-west, the thermometer falling rapidly to 7° or 8° below Zero: but when it shifts to any other quarter mild weather returns, and we have clear sunshine, with the thermometer frequently above 50° in the shade. Good roads, however, and good houses, are as yet wanting to render the winters of this country pleasant.

The sombre appearance of the forests, without a single evergreen to relieve the eye, and the total deficiency of verdure on the surface of the earth (for even the pastures hardly retain a trace of green), give a doleful aspect to the scenery at this season. The natural turf, in those spots where the shade is not too deep to allow a turf to be formed, is composed chiefly of annual grasses, or of such as wither down to the root in autumn: yet the perennial or evergreen species, which clothe the rich pastures of more northern climates with perpetual verdure, thrive here to admiration when sown even casually, and take entire possession of the soil, to the exclusion of the indigenous grasses. Where the little caravans have encamped as they crossed the prairies, and have given their cattle hay made of these perennial grasses, there remains ever after a spot of green turf for the instruction and encouragement of future improvers—a fact which, I think, is conclusive against the prevailing notion that the natural grasses, as they are called, are the best adapted to every soil and climate. Indeed, this opinion is at variance with experience in regard to almost every plant cultivated by man;

many of the grass tribe in particular, as wheat, barley, and oats, are every where exotics, or, more properly, such as we now see them, the creatures of art.

The wild grapes of this country are pleasant enough to invite us to introduce better, and denote a climate well adapted to the vine. The crab is inferior in size and flavour to ours in England; yet the cultivated apple exceeds any thing I have seen: in proof of the perfection which this fruit attains here, I have taken sixteen full-grown plump pippins from one apple. Pears also succeed very well. The peach bears fruit the third year from the stone; but the trees are short-lived and liable to blight. We have gooseberries and currants in perfection; and, in general, the vegetable productions of our old country, that have been introduced here, are improved by the change.

The season for sugar-making is now commencing; some has already been made in this neighbourhood. There are several species of the maple, from which sugar may be extracted. The hickery, and I believe some other trees, contain sugar of excellent quality; but the acer-saccharinum, or sugar-maple, affords the great supply of this article. In a favourable season (calm weather, frosty nights, and sunny days) I understand one hundred pounds of sugar may be collected from fifty trees; and one man, with great assiduity, may perform the work in about eight days, where the trees stand conveniently near to each other. Auger-holes are bored through the bark into the wood, about three feet from the ground, from which a tube, formed perhaps of cane, conveys the limpid and slightly sweet liquor into small troughs. Hard by, a range of iron kettles are steaming away; in these the " sugar water" is evaporated to a syrup of proper consistency. When in this state it is placed in a tub with holes in the bottom, and the process of graining (an imperfect chrystalization) is performed very handsomely, and a delicious molasses runs off through the holes. It is, however, generally grained very imperfectly in the kettles, by stirring it till it is cool. The great consumption of this article in Kentucky, Ohio, and Indiana, has been chiefly derived from the sugar-maple; but the cane is now cultivated with success in Louisiana, and cane-sugar in large quantities is brought up the river, and can be afforded cheaper, I believe, than that from the maple. The price this season, of the latter, is tweny-five cents per pound.

We are now feasting on wild turkeys. We have not sat down to dinner for the last month, I believe, without a fine roast turkey. They weigh about twelve pounds, and are sold five for a dollar.

Some weigh twenty-five pounds—I have heard of thirty. They are fat and tender; better, I fancy, than Norfolk turkeys: but I must not be too positive on this nice point.

You see the subjects which interest us Back-woods men, and they answer the purpose very well, in the room of the important matters that used to agitate us in England, grown still more important since we quitted, I suppose. I hear of loans to government, to pay the interest of which, I presume, you must have new taxes; I hear also of loans to parishes in aid of the poor-rates. Here we have now *no* taxes, excepting what are raised on the principle of our country rates, and they are hardly perceptible. The whole system of internal taxation is done away by a late act of Congress. Think of a country without excisemen, or as-sessors, or collectors, or receivers-general, or——— informers or paupers!

I ought to apologise for trifling at such a length, but this would add to the fault.

I am, &c.

P. S. I forgot to remark on the subject of our privations, as to all I had been used to know about government in our old country, that Congress, to save itself from total oblivion among the people, has, at the same time that it abolished taxes, de-

creed the distribution of certain sums for the improvement of the country, in canals, bridges, turn-
pikes, &c.

LETTER X.

MY DEAR SON,   *Jan.* 31, 1818.

I HAVE not, in any of my letters, given
you more than a general view of the advantages
attending a change, from your situation, for that of
an American farmer. This general knowledge of
the subject was all I had obtained myself; and
anxious as I am to communicate to you what I
know, I am still more so, to avoid misleading
you.

I have now, however, so far entered into the
details of our own establishment, that it would be
wrong any longer to withhold from you some particulars of our Illinois farming, as they lie practi-
cally before me. I shall give you an estimate of
expenditure and produce, on a section of land
such as I have now under my eye. The expenses
are put higher than the rates actually paid in this
country, and the produce on the whole, I believe,

within the average; so that you may rely on its being a safe statement.

When you have given it your attention, look around you for the cheapest and most eligible farm within your observation; make your calculations of capital employed, and of profit and loss, and then compare. It will soon be time for you to decide on your future settlement. I certainly wish that you may join us. What I feel on that point as your father; what we all feel when we indulge the hope of again embracing you; your own corresponding emotions of affection;—in making your decision, keep these considerations out of view: but if you conclude to follow us, give them full scope; and they will bear you up through the difficulties and discouragement which you will doubtless experience.

The course of cultivation which I have made the groundwork of the following calculations, may not turn out to be the best; but it is the most likely to succeed, under " existing circumstances," of any that has occurred to me.

It is customary to plant Indian corn on the first ploughing on newly broken up prairies, and the crop is left to struggle with the grass, which springs up abundantly between the furrows. Our method of skim-ploughing, I expect, will be found of great advantage, not only as regards this first

crop, but to the wheat which follows. Should it
prove that I am too sanguine in this particular,
the produce of the first crop is set too high; but
by way of compensation, you will observe that I
have entirely omitted the profits on live stock;
and it is on the boundless scope for rearing and
fattening hogs and cattle, that the farmers place
their chief reliance.

You will also observe, that the balance always
comes out an *even sum;* this is owing to the last
line of the list of expenses, which is merely an
allowance for incidents; and to ease the calculation, I have put that at such a sum as makes up
the *whole number*.

The farm is a section, or 640 acres, and consists of 240 acres wood, and 400 prairie. The
site of the house and farm-buildings, with garden,
orchard, and sundry other convenient inclosures,
are to be included in the 240 acres. The plan is
to break up 100 acres per annum; after which it
may be laid down to grass, or continued partly or
wholly arable, under this or any other course of
crops, as may be found expedient. The 100 acres
is to be planted with Indian corn in May, and
with wheat in October, after the Indian corn: thus
the whole 400 acres of prairie will be brought
into cultivation in four years.

A capital of £2,000 sterling (8,889 dollars)

may be invested on a section of such land, in the following manner: *viz.*

	Dollars.
Purchase of the land, 640 acres, at 2 dollars per acre	1,280
House and buildings, exceedingly convenient and comfortable, may be built for . .	1,500
A rail fence round the woods, 1,000 rods, at 25 cents per rod	250
About 1,800 rods of ditch and bank, to divide the arable into 10 fields, at 33⅓ . .	600
Planting 1,800 rods of live fence . .	150
Fruit-trees for orchard, &c. . . .	100
Horses and other live stock . . .	1,500
Implements and furniture . . .	1,000
Provision for one year, and sundry incidental charges	1,000
Sundry articles of linen, books, apparel, implements, &c. brought from England . .	1,000
Carriage of ditto, suppose 2,000 lb. at 10 dollars per cwt.	200
Voyage and travelling expenses of one person, suppose	309

Dollars 8,889

Note.—The first instalment on the land is 320 dollars, therefore 960 dollars of the purchase-money remain in hand, to be applied to the expenses of cultivation, in addition to the sums above stated.

Expenditure of first year.

	Dollars.
Breaking up 100 acres, 2 dollars per acre .	200
Indian corn for seed, 5 barrels (a barrel is 5 bushels)	10
Planting ditto	25
Horse-hoeing ditto, 1 dollar per acre . .	100
Harvesting ditto, 1½ dollar per acre . .	150
Ploughing the same land for wheat, 1 dollar per acre	100
Seed wheat, sowing, and harrowing . .	175
Incidental expenses	240
	1,000

Produce of first year.

100 acres Indian corn, 50 bushels (or 10 barrels) per acre, at 2 dollars per barrel . .	2,000
Net produce	1,000

Expenditure of second year.

Breaking up 100 acres for Indian corn, with expenses on that crop . . .	485
Harvesting and threshing wheat, 100 acres .	350
Ploughing 100 acres for wheat, seed, &c. .	275
Incidents	290
	1,400

Dollars.

Second year's expenditure brought forward   . 1,400

Produce of second year.

100 acres Indian corn, 10 barrels per   *Dollars.*
    acre, 2 dollars per barrel   .   2,000
100 acres wheat, 20 bushels per acre,
    3 dollars 75 cents per barrel   .   1,500 . 3,500

Net produce 2,100

Expenditure of third year.

Breaking up 100 acres as before, with expenses on crop of Indian corn . . .	485
Ploughing 100 acres wheat stubble for Indian corn	100
Horse-hoeing, harvesting, &c. ditto . .	285
Harvesting and threshing 100 acres wheat .	350
Dung-carting 100 acres for wheat, after second crop of Indian corn . . .	200
Ploughing 200 acres wheat, seed, &c. . .	550
Incidents	330
	2,300

Produce of third year.

200 acres Indian corn, 10 barrels per   *Dollars.*
    acre, 2 dollars per barrel   .   4,000
100 acres wheat, 20 bushels per acre,
    3 dollars 75 cents per barrel   .   1,500 . 5,500

Net produce 3,200

Expenditure of fourth year.

		Dollars·
As the third	2,300
Harvesting and threshing 100 acres more wheat .	350
Additional incidents	50
	2,700

Produce of fourth year.

	Dollars.	
200 acres Indian corn, as above .	4,000	
200 acres wheat . . .	3,000 .	7,000
	Net produce 4,300

Summary.

	Expenses. Dollars.	Produce. Dollars.
First year . .	1,000 .	2,000
Second . .	1,400 .	3,500
Third . . .	2,300 .	5,500
Fourth . . .	2,700 .	7,000
Housekeeping and other		18,000
expenses, four years . 4,000		11,400
Dollars 11,400		6,600

Net proceeds per ann. . .	1,650
Increasing value of land by cultivation and settlements, half a dollar per ann. on 640 acres . . .	320
	Annual clear profit 1,970

Housekeeping and other expenses being *paid*, there remains a profit of 22 per cent. on the capital, and you are improving your own estate.

Our market at the above prices, or exceeding them, I think is sure. The demand for grain will probably fully equal the produce for some years, owing to the influx of new settlers; and the southern states, down the Mississippi to New Orleans, will be an increasing and sure market for our surplus of every kind : vast quantities of pork and beef are shipped for New Orleans from Kentucky and Indiana. In this shape, that is, when applied to fattening cattle and hogs, we may *insure* two dollars per barrel for Indian corn.

LETTER XI.

(FROM AN ENGLISH EMIGRANT.)

SIR,   *Philadelphia, Dec.* 25, 1817.

HAVING perused your publication of a Tour through part of the United States, I am induced to write to you on the subject, being myself an English emigrant.

I wish particularly to be informed what an indigent emigrant will be paid for his labour, independent of what you propose to supply him with on his arrival at the new settlement; that is, what will his earnings be on the average annually? and what will be the annual rent of one of the cabins you propose building, with a cow and hog attached, and pasture for the same?

I have a wife and three children in England, which I intend sending for the ensuing spring. I had intended settling in the state of Ohio before seeing your publication, but am now more in favour of joining your proposed settlement, which appears to me very practicable.

I now wish to be informed which would be the most economical way of travelling with my family. Would it be possible for me to take a light waggon and one horse?

I calculate on being able to leave Philadelphia with 500 dollars. I am at present in the employ of Mr. . . . . Philadelphia, where you will have the goodness to address a letter to me.

I am, Sir, &c. &c.

P. S. I omitted informing you what profession I am: it is perhaps unnecessary; but I have from my infancy been reared a farmer.

LETTER XII.

(ANSWER TO THE PRECEDING.)

SIR,   *Jan.* 30, 1818.

Owing to some interruption in the mails, your letter did not reach me till this morning.

The large undertaking mentioned at the conclusion of my journal, is not yet in the way of execution. Proposals have been laid before Congress, (or at least transmitted to Washington for that purpose) but I expect no proceedings can be had without considerable delay, should they even be favourably received, which is extremely doubtful.

I am therefore going on steadily with my own settlement, without reference to that plan. Yet, in a smaller way, I shall make provision for the ease of settlers at the commencement of their labours, on the same principle.

I shall keep one or more cabins in readiness for new comers, and provide *immediately* for their employment. I cannot state to you with precision the earnings of a labouring man: I should suppose 230 dollars a year, from what I learn of prices now paid. I have abundant means of furnishing employment at that rate.

A cow and calf may cost from twelve to sixteen dollars; a breeding sow two or three dollars; these may be paid for out of their labour, by those who have not the means of purchasing. But their taking these, or any other necessaries which I may provide, will be altogether optional on their part. The rent of a cabin, with cow-house, pig-stye, well, and garden of one acre, with a right in a common meadow, and common pasture, equal to two acres in each, will not exceed twenty dollars a year; the tenant keeping the fence of his garden and his buildings in repair.

You might make your way from Philadelphia to Pittsburg with a light waggon; but from thence to the neighbourhood of our settlement, by far the cheapest and most easy mode of travelling is down the Ohio to Shawnee-town. At that place, which is fifty miles south of us, you would either take some land conveyance, or possibly might proceed up the Wabash to Harmony, or the mouth of Bonpas; which latter is about six miles from the south end of our prairie. You would, however, obtain at Shawnee-town information and advice as to your proceeding.

You may purchase a skiff at Pittsburg for six or seven dollars, which will bring you down the

Ohio in safety, with such instructions as you may collect on your passage.

If you conclude to join our settlement, you will, of course, write to me again before you leave Philadelphia.

You mention your having been reared a farmer, and your qualifications are of course well suited to our common occasions: but, above all, bring good morals, and then, with industry, barring the accidents to which we are ever liable, you must prosper.

I am, Sir,

your friend and well-wisher.

LETTER XIII.

DEAR SIR,   *Feb. 2*, 1818.

I HAVE not received a line from Europe from any of our friends, since they have been apprized of our establishment in the Illinois, so that whether you have quite given us up as wild adventurers, whom none but wild people will follow, or whether my explanation of our motives and views has produced a corresponding interest, and a

cordial sympathy in our success, is matter of speculation in our family circle, and adds no little to the
eagerness with which we anticipate packets that no
doubt are on their way. But however that may be,
our countrymen on this side of the Atlantic, many
of whom are now exploring this vast expanse of
wilderness, uncertain where to pitch their tents,
are becoming sensible of an attraction to this
point. I have numerous applications, both personal and by letter, and I think we have good
ground to expect that we may soon enjoy ourselves in a thriving neighbourhood.

Our district affords many eligible situations,
but it is unequal in quality of soil; and we have
such strong hold on the most desirable part of it,
that I flatter myself it will not be found sufficiently
inviting to land jobbers, who traverse this fine
country like a pestilent blight. Where they see
the promise of a thriving settlement, from a cluster
of entries being made in any neighbourhood, they
purchase large tracts of the best land, and lock it
up in real *mortmain*, for it is death to all improvement.

One of the greatest calamities to which a
young colony is liable is this investment of the
property of non-residents, who speculate on their
prosperity, whilst they are doing all they can to
impede it.

The wealth of the American merchants, collected as it is from the labours of their fellow-citizens of the wilderness, seldom returns to make that wilderness rejoice by converting it into a fruitful field, but is too commonly employed in retarding that happy change. This holding back from cultivation millions of acres, tends to scatter the population of these new countries; increasing the difficulties of settlers manifold; and occasioning the habits of savage life to be retained much longer. The western states are suffering greatly under this evil.

I have this day had the pleasure of a visit from a Kentish farmer, who will probably make one of our colony. He is returning to England *viâ* New Orleans, to fetch his family. His name is Clarke. I give him directions which I, hope will enable him to find you. He appears to be of the right sort, and you will have pleasure in communicating advice or assistance to him, should he need it, on re-shipping himself for this country. He left England in August last, in the ship Marianne of London, of 560 tons burthen, Captain James Johnson; Thomas and James Fitzgerald, brokers, St. Catharine's, Iron-gate Stairs; Gardiner, of Edmonton, owner. I am thus particular in names, on account of the patriotic proceedings I am going to relate to you.

This vessel was fitted up commodiously for passengers, especially of the steerage class. She was advertised as to sail for New York and Philadelphia, and printed bills to that effect were distributed. She took in two hundred passengers at twelve guineas a head, for a birth, fire, and water. Captain Johnson conducted her down the river and through the British Channel; he then found himself much indisposed, quitted the ship at Lymington, and Captain Jackson, who was there in readiness, took the command. About two days after Captain Jackson assumed his office, when they were off Scilly, he addressed his passengers, with " My honest friends! I suppose you know where you are going; we are bound to New Brunswick." You will imagine the rage and astonishment of these poor people; they would have proceeded to acts of immediate revenge and desperation, but were happily restrained by the influence of a few wise heads among them. When they had been a fortnight at sea, these same wise heads put them in the way of a remedy which proved in a great measure effectual. They presented to the captain, by common consent, a paper, which they called a petition, with which he thought it expedient to comply, so far as to carry them to Boston instead of New Brunswick. At Boston they laid their complaint before the British consul,

Mr. Skinner, demanding redress for the injury they sustained by being landed at that port, instead of New York or Philadelphia. Mr. Skinner declared himself incompetent, but advised them to *repair to New Brunswick*, where they might apply to real British authority and obtain ample justice; and moreover assured them, that on their arrival there they would each of them receive two hundred acres of land, and other advantages.

The kind of justice administered by the governor of New Brunswick in such cases, may be guessed from the practice of his neighbour at Halifax. Two vessels, under similar pretexts with the above, had just before obtained a living cargo of unfortunate persons, and actually landed them at that place, instead of the United States' port for which they had shipped themselves. They applied to the governor, but he was as incompetent as Mr. Skinner of Boston, and referred them to their mother-country. " *Return to England,*" said he, " there you will obtain *ample justice.*"

I call these transactions *patriotic ;* and if I am correct in the use of that epithet, the stamp of patriotism is on some or all of the names I have mentioned, and on the government, if it countenances such deeds. I had used another epithet; but I think patriotism, as exemplified in the practice of legitimate politicians, is sufficiently appropriate. It is *safe* too, as here explained: for I would by no means impute to these gentlemen, or to the government, patriotism of the American, or French, or even of the old English school.

We are waiting with some impatience for the season of commencing our farming operations. The horses are ready, and the ploughs and harness in a state of forwardness. We hope to begin work in March, and to be settled in May. Farming will be as good a business here, I think, as in England, with this difference, that instead of paying rent for our land, our land will pay rent to us, by its increasing value. There are a few other circumstances of difference with which you are acquainted, regarding tithes, taxes, and poor-rates. Labour, including that of horses, is somewhat lower than in England. Seventy-five cents, three shillings and fourpence halfpenny sterling, per day, is about the wages of a labouring man, boarding himself: but a man and two horses may be hired to plough at a dollar a day.

As I proceed to practice, I shall not fail to send you a fair, that is a true account. It will give me great pleasure to hear from you, and to have confirmed, under your hand, my hope of embracing you as a friend, a neighbour, and a fellow-citizen. We are all in excellent health: pray communicate our best wishes to the . . . . circle, and believe me

truly yours.

LETTER XIV.

MY DEAR SIR,   *Feb.* 15, 1818.

I HOPE you have received a long letter
which I despatched about four months ago, and
that the next mail will bring me one from you in
return. It is thus that by the glorious invention
of writing, of which I never before so fully felt
the value, the immensity of space which divides us
from our friends may be reduced to its original
nothing: for if I were re-established in my old
armed-chair at Wanborough, and you remaining
in yours, we should, in point of fact, be separated
as completely as we are at this moment.

We shall not be entirely settled in our own
home, beyond the Wabash, before the beginning
of May, a period which we anticipate with much
pleasure. The Indiana side of that river has the
start of the Illinois about three years, which makes
a vast difference in the state of things to a near
observer, but to you it is one and the same country; and a residence of seven months, on one side
or the other, has now given me some title to be
accounted an inhabitant. The interest I feel in
every person and thing that surrounds me is
naturally very great, not only from the novelty of

the situation, but because it is that in which I hope and believe I am to pass the remainder of my days.   We have just had our assizes : the circuit court, similar to our court of assize, was held last week, the second time since our arrival.   I wish I could introduce you to " his honour" the judge ; to the gentlemen of the jury ; to the learned brethren who fill the parts both of solicitor and counsel ; to the assemblage of spectators, all males, for women never attend the courts except on business ; and even to the accomplished villains who are here exposed to public indignation, far more terrific than the vengeance of the law.

In this early stage of society, where the country is savage, and many of the people but just emerging from that condition, much intrepidity of mind and hardihood of body are indispensable requisites in the administration of justice.   *Brass* for the face wont suffice, they must be *steel* from head to foot.

Your military or fox-hunting experience has, I dare say, furnished adventures similar to those which are constantly occurring here to the gentlemen of the long robe, on their progress from court to court. The judge and the bar are now working their way to the next county seat, through almost trackless woods, over snow and ice, with the thermometer about Zero.   In last November circuit the judge swam his horse, I think, seven times in one day; how often in the whole circuit is not in the record. What would our English lawyers say to seven such ablutions in one November day? and then to dry their clothes on their back by turning round and round before a blazing fire, preparatory to a night's lodging on a cabin floor wrapped in their blankets; which, by the by, are the only robes used by the profession here.

I have an anecdote of a judge with whom I am well acquainted, and therefore I believe it. I give it you as an instance of intrepidity, as well as of that ferocious violence which occurs but too frequently; by no means, however, as a specimen of the judicial character. A few years ago, before he was advanced to his present dignity, the foreman of a grand jury insulted him outrageously, out of court of course. The man had a large knife in his hand, such as hunters always carry about them, and well know the use of; but the enraged barrister, with a hand-whip, or cow-hide as they are called, laid on so keenly that he actually cut his jacket to ribbons in defiance of the knife; and when the beaten and bleeding juryman made his piteous case known to his brethren, they fined him a dozen of wine for his cowardice.

Another anecdote. A notorious offender had escaped from confinement, and, mounted on a capital horse, paraded the town where the judge resided, with a brace of loaded pistols, calling at the stores and grog-shops, and declaring he would shoot any man who should attempt to molest him. The judge hearing of it, loaded a pistol, walked deliberately up to the man to apprehend him, and on his making show of resistance shot him immediately. The ball entered the breast and came out behind, but did not prove mortal. He fell, was reconducted to gaol, escaped a second time, and was drowned in crossing the Ohio.

Judges are appointed by the legislature for the term of seven years. Salary, seven hundred dollars per annum; a sum which is certainly inadequate, even in this cheap country. It will, however, be increased as wealth and population increase: the office is honourable to a man of talents and integrity, and may open the road to more lucrative appointments.

My personal knowledge of the gentlemen of the law is not, I fear, a fair criterion of their general character. I have seen many proofs of candour, high principle, and correct judgement. There are lawyers here whom no sum would bribe to undertake a mean business; but I hear of chicanery in some, and have perceived strong symptoms of vice and dissipation in others.

The tendency of the profession, here as in

England, and I suppose every where, is to increase the baseness of little, cunning, avaricious
minds; and the pestilent example and society of
the idle and corrupt, have the same baneful influence over inexperienced young men who are
exposed to it.

As companions to my anecdotes of the judge,
I must give you some traits of an honest young
lawyer of my acquaintance. Three years ago he
made his appearance as a candidate for practice,
in a home-spun coat, and probably without a
dollar in his pocket. He was called " the home-
spun lawyer." His father, a plain farmer, had
given him as good an education as he could afford,
and on his quitting the parental roof to commence
his professional career, wishing him to make a
figure suitable to his new character, he desired
him to call at the store where he usually dealt,
and furnish his wardrobe to his own liking. The
young man thought of his brothers and sisters, and
of the expense which had been incurred in his education, and supposed he might have already received his share; so passing the store, he resolved
to rub on in home-spun clothes until he had earned
better, which soon happened—and they *wore well*.

His practice increased, and his reputation with
it: the second year, he obtained the office of state-
attorney for the county, with the salary of one

hundred dollars! In the course of the year, his
exertions in bringing to justice an offender merited
a further recompense, in the opinion of a man interested in the case, and who could well afford to
give it. This gentleman offered him fifty dollars
as a present. The young man hesitated: he had
done no more than his duty in quality of attorney-
general, and for that he was paid by the public.
He examined the law: no prohibition appeared to
his accepting an additional fee. The sum was
tempting; it was as much as £500 to the man
who receives a salary of £1000; still he could
not be satisfied that it was his due, and he finally
refused it.

This year he was chosen by his fellow-citizens
to represent them in the state-legislature, from
which duty he has just returned; and, if prosperity
does not spoil him, the home-spun lawyer will be
an honour to his father, and useful to his country.

I shall spare you, for the present, an introduction to any of the remaining personages who composed our court. Our friend . . . . . to whom I
would be most kindly remembered, will be amused
at the amount of the judges' and attorneys' salaries.
Should his ambition be excited, I am sorry to say
he would have but a poor chance of success, for I
believe, from one end of the union to the other,
every department of law is crowded almost to suf-
focation.

We have had an unusually severe winter: the mercury has once been 12° below Zero, and several times approaching that extreme. At present the weather is delightful, the thermometer just above freezing, and the air clear and serene. We are told that there will be but little more cold weather.

I remain sincerely yours.

LETTER XV.

DEAR SIR,   *Feb.* 24, 1818.

WHEN a man gives advice to his friends, on-affairs of great importance to their interest, he takes on himself a load of responsibility, from which I have always shrunk, and generally withdrawn. My *example* is very much at their service, either for imitation or warning, as the case may be.

I must however in writing to *you*, step a little over this line of caution, having more than once been instrumental in helping you, not *out* of your difficulties, but from one scene of perplexity to another; I cannot help advising you to make an effort more, and extricate yourself and family, completely, by removing into this country.

When I last saw you, twelve months ago, I did not think favourably of your prospects : if things have turned out better, I shall be rejoiced to hear it, and you will not need the advice I am preparing for you. But, if vexation and disappointments have assailed you, as I feared ; and you can honourably make your escape, with the means of transmitting yourself hither, and one hundred pounds sterling to spare,—don't hesitate.

In six months after I shall have welcomed you, barring accidents, you shall discover that you are become *rich*, for you shall feel that you are independent; and I think that will be the most delightful sensation you ever experienced : for you will receive it multiplied as it were by the number of your family, as your troubles now are.

It is not, however, a sort of independence that will excuse you from labour, or afford you many luxuries, that is, costly luxuries. I will state to you what I have learnt, from a good deal of observation and inquiry, and a little experience ; then you will form your own judgment.

In the first place, the voyage.—That will cost, to Baltimore or Philadelphia, provided you take it, as no doubt you would, in the cheapest way, twelve guineas each, for a birth, fire, and water, for yourself and wife, and half price or less for your children; besides provisions, which you will furnish.

Then the journey.—Over the mountains to Pittsburgh, down the Ohio to Shawnee-town, and from thence to our settlement, fifty miles north, will amount to five pounds sterling per head.

If you arrive here as early as May, or even June, another five pounds per head will carry you on to that point, where you may take your leave of dependence on any thing earthly but your own exertions.

At this time I suppose you to have remaining one hundred pounds (borrowed probably from English friends, who rely on your integrity; and who may have directed the interest to be paid to me on their behalf, and the principal in due season).

We will now, if you please, turn it into dollars, and consider how it may be disposed of.   A hundred pounds sterling will go a great way in dollars.   With eighty dollars you will " enter a quarter section of land;" that is, you will purchase at the land-office one hundred and sixty acres, and pay one-fourth of the purchase-money; and looking to the land to reward your pains with the means of discharging the other three-fourths as they become due, in two, three, and four years.

You will build a house with fifty dollars; and you will find it extremely comfortable and convenient, as it will be really and truly yours.

Two horses will cost, with harness and plough, one hundred.

Cows, and hogs, and seed corn, and fencing, with other expenses, will require the remaining two hundred and ten dollars.

This beginning, humble as it appears, is affluence and splendor, compared with the original outfit of settlers in general. Yet no man remains in poverty, who possesses even moderate industry and economy, and especially of *time*.

You would of course bring with you your sea-bedding and store of blankets, for you will need them on the Ohio; and you should leave England with a good stock of wearing apparel. Your luggage must be composed of light articles, on account of the costly land-carriage from the eastern port to Pittsburg, which will be from seven to ten dollars per 100 lb. nearly sixpence sterling per pound.

A few simple medicines of good quality are indispensable, such as calomel, bark in powder, castor oil, calcined magnesia, and laudanum: they may be of the greatest importance on the voyage and journey, as well as after your arrival.

Change of climate and situation will produce temporary indisposition, but with prompt and judicious treatment, which is happily of the most simple kind, the complaints to which new comers are liable are seldom dangerous or difficult to overcome, provided due regard has been had to salubrity in the choice of their settlement, and to diet and accommodation after their arrival. With best regards,

I remain, &c.

LETTER XVI.

(TO A FRIEND IN FRANCE.)

MY DEAR SIR,   *Feb.* 28, 1818.

I LEFT England a month earlier than I had calculated on. The importance of the undertaking had rendered me proportionably industrious in preparing for it; thus I found myself in a state of forwardness with my little arrangements, that enabled me to accept the offer of an agreeable captain, with the entire accommodations of a fine vessel. This made the voyage easy, and even pleasant, to the females of our party. Before my departure I put your commission in good train, as I hope you discovered.

It was not until I arrived in this remote region that I saw the great utility of the lithographic art,

and, when it was too late, I regretted that we did
not bring out such a knowledge of it as might be
applied to practice: if we had the art in detail, we
should find artists.   Many objects of natural history are constantly presenting themselves, which
this would enable us to preserve by drawings, and
communicate *ad libitum* to our distant friends.   It
is peculiarly adapted to the state of things here,
and I shall avail myself of your friendship in order
to obtain it for our infant colony.

You will receive this through my bookseller
in London, with a small volume, giving some particulars of this country, and of our pilgrimage.
From it you will learn where we are, and I hope
you will, as early as possible, put it in my power
to aid your economical museum.   The catalogue
and list of desiderata you promised me, must now
be forwarded by way of Philadelphia.

We are here in the substantial enjoyment of
those rights, which have been torn from *you* before you well understood their value; and which
my unhappy country has relinquished one by one,
under the fond hope of saving the remainder: like
the crew of a sinking ship throwing overboard the
cargo.

Liberty is no subject of dispute or speculation
among us Back-woods men: it is the very atmosphere we breathe.   I now find myself the fel-

low-citizen of about nine millions of persons, who
are affording a sober and practical confutation of
those base men, who would pass for philosophers,
and have dared to call this unalienable birthright
of every human being a visionary scheme.

In passing from theory to practice, I have experienced no diminution of my love for freedom;
but I hate tyranny more cordially, and I want
language to express the loathing I feel for personal slavery: practised by freemen it is most de-
testable. It is the leprosy of the United States;
a foul blotch which more or less contaminates the
entire system, in public and in private, from the
president's chair to the cabin of the hunter.

It is not the states alone where slavery is
established by law, that are suffering under this
outrageous insult upon humanity; the bitter in-
heritance of former injustice exists in all, in the
profligacy of the black population, the free people
of colour, degraded in public opinion (and therefore degraded and depraved in character) by the
complexion which the God of nature has given
them. It is also exemplified even in the eastern
states, as I am informed, where the practice of
keeping slaves has been long discontinued, in er-
roneous notions of the relations of master and
servant, in a way which interferes greatly with
domestic comfort.

In the slave states, the negro is not the only object of commiseration: I have learnt, from the most unquestionable testimony, that every class of the white population is more or less corrupted by idleness, extravagance, and debauchery. These evils are generally acknowledged and deplored, and it is probable that, ere many years have passed, a remedy, mild as the case will admit, must be applied by a wise and strong legislature; or some dreadful eruption will bring about a cure, arising out of the evil itself.

When my thoughts turn towards Europe, which you may well suppose to be their prevailing bias, it is not this lamentable flaw in the political and domestic system of our republic which can prevent my longing to see around me, and partaking of the good which so much preponderates, many estimable friends who remain under difficulties far greater than those we have escaped from.

How fare those friends whom I had the pleasure of seeing first at your house, and from whom I afterwards experienced so much kindness? How gladly would I prepare a refuge for them here! These are not words of course, meaning nothing, or nothing beyond civility. I have both the will and the means of providing a home for them, should they need it; and at all events, I could aid them in establishing themselves. And our excellent friend the Abbé ———, and the family at the Grange: how admirably this climate would suit them. You would gratify me much by giving me their news, and also by presenting to them my most cordial remembrances. Great distance, instead of slackening, draws tighter the attachments of good men, a rank which it is baseness not to aspire to: allow me, therefore, to consider my acquaintance with you in Europe to be improved into friendship, now that I am an Illinois farmer. Under this impression I not only tax you with this long letter, but I beg to hear from you when you can find a conveyance for Philadelphia. Four of my family are with me, two sons and two daughters, who will all be Americans.

I am yours sincerely.

LETTER XVII.

(TO A GENTLEMAN OF PHILADELPHIA.)

SIR,   *March* 2, 1818.

I HAVE only this day received your letter of December 25, owing to interruptions in the carriage of the mails, which have incommoded us greatly.

I shall reply to your inquiries as they occur. The first materials for the buildings on a new settlement in this country are, almost without exception, logs.

The plan generally adopted, by those who propose eventually to establish themselves in brick, is to construct such log cabins for their temporary abode, as may afterwards be applicable to other useful purposes.

The expense of these, as of all other buildings, is in a great degree optional; you may make them snug and agreeable dwellings.

A range of cabins I am now preparing for my family will contain ten apartments. The mere building is performed by contract for two hundred and fifty dollars; when finished they will cost about eight hundred dollars; but the doors and windows, and the floors and ceilings (both of plank), are to form a part of our future habitation.

We have lime-stone and sand-stone suitable for building, and plenty of brick earth; thus we abound in excellent materials. Labourers may now be procured at from seventy-five cents to one dollar per day; but I presume, the number is so small, that new comers must not rely on obtaining them at that price, unless emigrants of that description accompany them.

Household furniture is to be procured at a moderate price, and pretty well made. The woods furnish cherry and black walnut, and probably various other kinds of timber suitable for cabinet-making; and workmen of that description are not very rare. Beds and bedding should be brought out. Kitchen furniture is found at the stores. Groceries in general have been received from your city or Baltimore, now they come from New Orleans: coffee is about forty cents per pound; sugar, from twenty-two to fifty cents; tea, two dollars fifty cents; salt is found or made in abundance, and of good quality, in various parts of the western country. Vast quantities of pork and beef are cured for the southern market.

The demand for all the necessaries of life increases so rapidly, that the supply does not always keep pace with it; and those who want money or foresight are sometimes compelled to pay high prices. High prices stimulate the producer, supply is increased, and the articles soon recover their due level, until a similar cause operates in again occasioning a temporary scarcity. Thus salt, which might be afforded at seventy-five cents per bushel, now sells at two dollars and upwards.

On the subject of lands in our neighbourhood, my engagements to my friends preclude my offering you any that I have taken up, but I shall be happy to give you such information, on your visit into this country, as I have obtained.

I would certainly advise you, as you suggest, to bring with you store of garden seeds, they are light and not bulky; and though many useful vegetables are met with in the gardens here, their seeds are not to be got with so. little trouble as bringing them.

Steam-boats are beginning to ply on the Wabash; and before many months, our river will probably turn out one or more of her own.

If you have serious intentions of settling in this part of the western country, you will first visit it of course. You may rely on my desire to give you every assistance which my situation will allow.

I am, Sir,

your obedient servant.

LETTER XVIII.

(TO AN ENGLISH GENTLEMAN NOW IN AMERICA.)

SIR,   *March 2,* 1818.

I HAVE only this day received your letter of the 24th December, owing to an excessive derangement in the mail department of this western country, which, however, is now likely to meet with adequate correction.

Though a stranger to you, I am greatly interested in the account you give of your sentiments and views, and shall feel sincere pleasure in promoting the latter.

For this end, I recommend your visiting our infant settlement as early as you can this spring. You may go from Philadelphia by stage to Pittsburg, from thence the Ohio will conduct you to Shawnee-town, where you will be directed to us. The distance from Shawnee-town to our prairie is about fifty miles.

There are continual opportunities of passing down the Ohio, which is certainly the easiest and cheapest mode of travelling; but you may perhaps prefer taking the journey from Pittsburg on horseback as we did, in which case I would advise you to take the same route; viz. by Wheeling to Chilicothe and Cincinnati, from thence through Indiana to Vincennes.

This would afford you an extensive view of the country, and enable you to form comparisons that might contribute to your final satisfaction and contentment in the choice that you shall make. This is a consideration worthy your attention.

Every situation on this globe, I believe, has its disadvantages, a something which you would wish otherwise. There are, moreover, as you are well aware, very many small privations inseparable from the condition of early settlers; and a journey of five hundred miles through the woods of Ohio and Indiana is excellent discipline for an inhabitant of an old country, preparatory to his assuming that character. He will be capable of appreciating his advantages of situation, and will not be so apt to attribute inconveniences, which he could escape no where, to local evils of his own (as he would then deem it) unhappy lot.

Many people spend the best part of their lives in roaming over this vast country in quest of a happy spot, which they never find; flying from nuisances which might be removed, or obviated, or even supported with half the labour and suffering they experience in making their escape from them, into circumstances probably as bad or worse.

I invite you to see the spot where we have pitched our tent; and I sincerely hope that you may fix yours in our neighbourhood, and that we may be serviceable and agreeable to each other, finding a cheerful retreat from the bustle of the world, of which I am as weary, I presume, as you are. Taking all things into consideration, I prefer

it to any I have seen or heard of, and looking
at it now with a favourable eye, as I wish to
do, I see new advantages continually arising before me.

In reply to your inquiry about the disposal of
part of the lands I have entered, I think you may
suit yourself as well at the land-office as by taking
such as I could spare, even at the government
price.

I have sons to settle, for whom I wish to reserve farms near to mine; and I have made particular engagements with some few other individuals whom I expect from England, which I think
will leave nothing very eligible at present in my
power to offer you.

The earlier your visit, the better will be your
opportunity of selection, as the public attention is
turned considerably towards our district.

Should you, as you hint, come round by New
Orleans, Shawnee-town is still your landing-place.
Your voyage up from New Orleans, by steam,
will be about a month. Steam-boats are passing
continually. A gentleman, who is just come down
the Ohio, saw ten new ones on the stocks at different ports on the river.

You inquire what commission I should charge
if I purchased land for you? If funds are provided, I dare say the commission is moderate; no

doubt there is a customary charge, but I have not heard it. It would be a task I should undertake with reluctance, to choose a situation for another, but my *opinion* you shall have *gratis*. If I purchase for *you*, being a matter of business, I should make the customary demand upon you for my services; and on this point I shall take care to inform myself and you of the amount before a step is taken.

I am, Sir,

your friend and servant.

LETTER XIX.

DEAR SIR,   *March* 18, 1818.

I HAVE received from Mr. ———, of Philadelphia, a credit for six hundred pounds sterling on your account; and by a letter from Mr. ———, I learn that it is your wish that I should invest that sum in land for you in the neighbourhood of our settlement: it is very agreeable to me to receive this commission, though (for reasons which I shall explain to you on some part of this large sheet) I shall not execute it.

It shews me that your heart is with us, and that you will follow in due season, when that tie shall be loosened which filial duty will not allow you to sever. In the mean time there will be collecting, on and around our " English prairie," a society which I am already enjoying by anticipation.

In this country they build " cob houses;" a " cob " is the interior part of a head of Indian corn after the grains are stripped off; with these cobs, which are lying about every where, structures are raised by the little half Indian brats, very much like our " houses of cards," whose chief merit lies in their tumbling down before they are finished; or like castles in the air, which are built by most people in every country *under the age of fifty.*

But my anticipations regarding our English prairie, are neither cob houses, nor card houses; nor, I think, castles in the air, for the last weighty reason, the age of the architect: and for a reason still more substantial, viz. our social building is begun on a firm and good foundation, and with good materials.

And now I come (quitting all metaphor) to your commission. I will purchase for you a *section* of land, 640 acres, for which I shall give, by paying the whole amount down, only 1036 dollars, or 1 dollar 62 cents per acre; and the remain-

der of your remittance I shall hold at your disposal, to purchase land if you please *where we do
not desire to see inhabitants.* This section I shall
reserve for you, in the full belief that you will
come and settle amongst us.   If I were to lay out
the whole six hundred pounds in the usual way of
entering land, by paying the first instalment of
half a dollar per acre, it would cover more than
eight square miles; and on your arrival a few years
hence to take possession of your estate, instead of
finding yourself in a circle of perhaps thirty prosperous families, you would have to settle in a de-
sert of your own creating.   Had I executed half
the commissions of this kind which have been proposed to me, I must have contented myself with
" cob houses," instead of those delightful and reasonable hopes of a happy society round our English prairie, in which I believe no one can sympa-
thize more fully than yourself.

I don't want an Agrarian law to define the limit
of every man's estate; but it is plain that if we
pre-occupy the land, we must live by ourselves.
Our colony must, to be prosperous, or indeed to
have an existence worthy the name, be composed
of persons who own the land they cultivate, and
cultivate the lands they own.   If any of us have
funds to spare, and choose to invest them in land,
it must not be on our own settlement.   I have

taken up far more than I have any intention of retaining, merely to exclude speculations which would frustrate our views.

If Mr. ———, has not embarked before this reaches you, I request you to inform him that I decline a compliance with his wish, which was communicated to me at the same time with yours, for the same reasons. On his arrival he will, I doubt not, see the propriety of my conclusion, which is formed on the supposition of his and your intention being to *hold* these large tracts as permanent estates. If he thinks differently from me, he will of course pursue his own plan, and also communicate to you his reasons, and then if you choose you can do the like.

Our application to Congress has not succeeded, which renders it more desirable to make room for our countrymen, many of whom are directing their steps to this place.

I wrote to you in June, in November, and again in January. The November letter gave you a pretty circumstantial detail of my own plans, and in particular I informed you of the size of my intended farm, which would seem inconsistent with the sentiments I have just expressed. But I hope soon to be reduced within moderate limits, by providing farms out of that tract for some of my sons: when I have laid off good farms for them, my actual occupation will be confined, as I now wish it to be, to a very moderate extent.

A naval establishment occupies our attention at present. We Americans must have a navy. We are forming two pirogues out of large poplars, with which we propose to navigate the Wabash; by lashing them together, and laying planks across both, we shall have a roomy deck, besides good covered stowage in both, and take a bulky as well as a heavy cargo. And we hope to have a shipping port at the mouth of Bonpas, a considerable stream which falls into the Wabash at the point where the latter makes a bold bend to the west, and approaches within a few miles of our prairie.

The subject of advancing the price of public lands has been before Congress.

I shall annex the report of a committee, to which it was referred, and which was acceded to. It contains interesting details, and general information of great importance.

A space exceeding, perhaps tenfold, the amount of lands in cultivation, still remains unappropriated; and such is the natural anxiety to possess land, and the facility with which that inclination may be satisfied in this country (a state of things likely to remain much the same for ages), that here will always be a scarcity of efficient circulating capital, which is valuable in proportion to its scarcity.

The merchant invests his profits, and the professional man his savings, in the purchase of uncultivated lands. The farmer, instead of completing the improvement of his present possessions, lays out all he can save in entering more land. In a district which is settling, this speculation is said to pay on the average, when managed with judgment, fifteen per cent. Who then will submit to the toils of agriculture, further than bare necessity requires, for fifteen per cent? Or who would loan his money, even at fifteen per cent, when he can obtain that interest by investing it in land? Thus every description of men, almost every man, is poor in convertible property.

I think this country affords abundant opportunities of applying capital more profitably, as well as more agreeably, than in the possession of large tracts of uncultivated land. Take as much of it as you can use and enjoy, but no more. Keep your capital in activity, and within your power; and you will soon see that two dollars of ready money are worth more than an acre of wilderness.

These are impressions made on my mind by surrounding circumstances, and if they prove cor-

rect, it will be good for us in our new settlement
to be influenced by them.

I remain, dear Sir,

sincerely yours.

Report of the Committee on Public Lands, on the
  subject of increasing the price at which the
  lands of the United States shall hereafter be
  sold.

Jan. 5, 1818.

The Committee on the Public Lands, to whom
was referred a resolution instructing them to inquire into the expediency of increasing the price
at which the public lands shall be sold hereafter,
have had the same under consideration, and respectfully report :—

That the lands of the United States are care-
fully surveyed, and divided into sections of 640
acres, quarter sections, and in certain cases eighths
of sections; that they are advertised for, and set
up at public sale, and disposed of to the highest
bidder at any price above two dollars per acre;
if they are not sold they are returned to the
register's office, and may be entered for, in the
office, at two dollars per acre, with a credit, after
the payment of one-fourth, of two, three, and four

years; the effects of this part of the system has been heretofore deemed beneficial, both to the public and to individuals. It is beneficial to individuals, because the price is so moderate, that the poorest citizen may place himself in the most useful and honourable situation in society, by becoming a cultivator of his own land:—and the fixed value is so high, connected with the abundance of our vacant territory, as to prevent individuals from purchasing, with a hope of advantage, unreasonably extensive and numerous tracts, to be held for purposes of speculation. That this is the case, that lands sold by the United States are not held by speculators, may be fairly inferred by a consideration of the following facts :—From the opening of the land offices in the north-west territory, as it was then called, to the 30th September, 1810, 3,167,829 acres of land were sold; this amount, compared with the population in 1810, is in the ratio of something less than twelve acres for each individual; the free white inhabitants of Virginia in 1800 amounted to 518,674, the lands of the state valued in 1798 amounted to 40,458,644 acres; this divided among the inhabitants, gives to each individual upwards of 76 acres of land: but it will not be contended that the lands of Virginia are held by speculators; and with much less truth can it be so said of the lands north-west of the Ohio.

Again, to shew by inference that the public lands are not disposed of at too low a price, the committee have thought proper to inquire into the estimated value of the lands in several of the states; and they find, that in the year 1788 the lands of New Hampshire, amounting to 3,749,061 acres, were valued at 19,028,108 dollars, or 5 dollars, 7 cents per acre.

In Pennsylvania, 11,959,865 acres were valued at 62,824,852 dollars, or 6 dollars, 9 cents per acre.

In Maryland, 5,444,272 acres, were valued at 21,634,004 dollars, or 3 dollars, 77 cents per acre.

In Virginia, 40,458,644 acres, were valued at 59,976,860 dollars, or 1 dollar, 48 cents per acre; and finally, in the sixteen states, at that time composing the United States, the land amounted to 163,746,686 acres, valued at 479,293,263 dollars, or 2 dollars, 92 cents per acre. Now if the lands of the United States, settled and peopled as they were, have been thus valued, it may safely be concluded that the uninhabited wilds of our forests are not disposed of at too low a price.

Indeed the Committee feel somewhat apprehensive that the United States, so far from being enabled to increase, will find themselves compelled to lessen the price of the public lands, or to forego the golden dreams they indulge in of enor-

mous revenue to arise from their sale. It will
be recollected by the house, that heretofore the
public has been the monopolist of land; that notwithstanding this advantage, not more than eight
or nine millions of acres have been disposed of
for a sum less than 19,000,000 of dollars, and
that too during a space of eighteen or twenty
years.

They will now take into consideration the fact,
that five or six millions of acres have been given
as bounty to the soldiers of the late war, and now
are, or soon will be, in the market, to meet the demands which the United States alone could heretofore supply. The committee will not obtrude
upon the house the deductions or reflections
which grow out of this state of things; they content themselves with the justification it affords of
the resolution which they respectfully submit.

Resolved, that it is inexpedient at the present
time to increase the price at which the public lands
are required to be sold.

LETTER XX.

MY DEAR FRIEND,   *March* 23, 1818.

As the spring comes on, our colony be_ gins to assume a most encouraging aspect.   I am employed with delight inexpressible in preparing a place of refuge for many a one, " of whom"— shall I say it?—" the world," such a world as we have escaped from, " was not worthy."

Our English friends are gathering round us; and so far from being solitary, and doleful, and desolate in this remote region, you must reverse all this to form any notion of our condition.

The toil and the difficulty, and even the dangers, attending the removal of a family from the hills of Surrey to the prairies of Illinois are consider- able: and the responsibility is felt at every step, a load upon the spirits of a father, for which his honest intentions are not at all times a sufficient counterpoise.   To have passed through all this harmless, and even triumphantly, to have secured a retreat for ourselves, and then, turning our backs upon care and anxiety, to be employed in smoothing the way, and preparing a happy rest- ing place for other weary pilgrims, is an enjoyment which I did not calculate upon when we quitted our old home.

" A lodge in some vast wilderness" was the exchange we contemplated ; fortifying our minds against the privations we were to experience, by a comparison with the evils we hoped to retire from : and now, instead of burying ourselves in a boundless forest, among wild animals, human and brute, we are taking possession of a cheerful abode, to be surrounded by well informed and prosperous neighbours. How sincerely do I wish you and yours could be among them, without the pain of moving and the perils of the journey! Foolish as it is, to wish for what we know cannot be accomplished.

It is a matter of curious speculation, collecting as we are from the four winds of Heaven as it were, what our society is to be in regard to religious *demonstrations.* In the region we are to inhabit, " the sun shineth" not " upon the just, and upon the unjust;" but upon the earth, and the trees, and the wild animals, as it shone before man was created.

There is nothing in the spirit of the government, nor in the institutions of this western country, nor in the habits of the people, which gives preponderancy to any sentiment on this subject of social religion, but that of abhorrence of priestly domination, and of all assumption of authority in these matters.

Now, having this " upward road" thus clear before us, when we shall have settled ourselves in our cabins, and fixed ourselves to our minds as to this world, what sort of a garb, think you, shall we assume as candidates for the next?—To my very soul I wish that we might assume none, —but the character of men who desire to keep their conscience void of offence towards God and towards man:—" *Nil conscire sibi, nullâ pallescere culpâ.*"   Another foolish wish! you will say. We shall have people among us, I dare say, who will undertake to teach religion; the most arro-gant of all pretensions, I should be apt to call it, had not frequent observation convinced me that it has no necessary connection with arrogance of character.   But however that may be, teachers, no doubt, will arise among us.—This most sensi-tive nerve has been touched, and already I have had the pleasure of two communications on the subject of religious instruction; both from stran-gers.

One of them, who dates from New Jersey, writes as follows.   " I have read your notes on a " journey from the coast of Virginia to the Illi-" nois territory; and I sincerely wish you success " in every laudable undertaking.—The religion of

" Jesus Christ, disentangled from the embarrass-
" ments of every sect and party, I hope you will
" encourage to the utmost of your power and abi-
" lities. In the genuine, uncorrupted, native, and
" pure spring of the Gospel, you view the world
" as your country, and every man as your brother.
" In that you will find the best security and gua-
" rantee of virtue and good morals, and the main
" spring of civil and religious liberty," &c. &c.—
As this gentleman's good counsel was not coupled
with any tangible proposition, his letter did not
call for a reply; in fact, the writer did not favour
me with his address.

My other zealous, though unknown friend,
who dates still more to the north than New Jersey, informs me that many are coming west, and
that he wants to come himself if he can " pave the
way." " We must," he says, " have an Unitarian
" church in your settlement, wherever it may be,
" and I will, if I live, come and open it. I am using
" every means in my power to promote the prin-
" ciples in . . . . . and ultimately to raise a congre-
" gation, and give, if possible, a mortal stab to infi-
" delity and bigotry." To this gentleman I replied
as follows :—' As to your idea of coming out in the
' character of a minister, I have not a word to say,
' dissuasive or encouraging. For myself I am of
' no sect, and generally in my view those points

'by which sects are distinguished are quite
'unimportant, and might be discarded without
'affecting the essence of true religion.   I am, as
'yourself, a foe to bigotry; but it is a disease for
'which I think no remedy is so effectual as letting
'it alone, especially in this happy country, where
'it appears under its mildest character, without
'the excitements of avarice and ambition.'—So
endeth the first chapter, of the first book, of our
ecclesiastical history.

A *third* foolish wish is at the very point of
my pen; but I withhold it, or I don't know
what might come to pass. . . . .
.   .   .   .

I remain, my dear friend,

ever affectionately yours.

LETTER XXI.

MY DEAR ——,   *March* 26, 1818.

It is too long an interval between the departure of a letter, and the arrival of a reply, for
me to refrain from writing to you.   In truth,

questions and answers six months apart can rarely
meet properly; so it is as well to give up the idea
of *dialogue* in our correspondence, except as to
plain substantial matter of fact. I hardly look
forward now to seeing you here; yet I *am* to have
that pleasure, though it seems put off to a distance
beyond my ken; but being deferred by causes in
which I most cordially rejoice, I cannot wish it
otherwise. . . . .
. . . .

Difficulties and privations—on these we reckoned;
but we trust the rudest are past, and we foresee
much satisfaction in overcoming and supplying
the remainder. For myself, so busy am I in plans
and preparations, that I fancy young hope has visited my age, for life seems again new to me. My
daughters give you all our family history; so,
now let me chat with you on subjects that will
suffer nothing by a month or two of delay.—Old
General Scott, the late governor of Kentucky,
whose name is coupled with many a pleasant anecdote, to cap the marvellous tales of some boast-
ing youths, said he had once met with a log so
crooked, that it could not lie still! I think there
are many such logs in England. But let them
alone; they are unworthy of notice,—those crooked, calumniating tempers! We are happily beyond
their reach. I trust our good name will not suf-

fer by their malevolence, and if we deserved a bad one it would be sure to follow us; for " it is hard," as we say in this country, " for a bird to fly away from its tail."

Emigration to the extreme limits of this western America will not repair a bad character. If a man would recover a lost reputation, let him reform, and remain at home. In no part of the world, I believe, is it more difficult to *assume* the position of an honest and correct man, with a tainted reputation.   There are people in England so uninformed of the state of society here, as to imagine that men may abscond for their misdeeds in that country, and be received in this as though nothing had happened : but the best they can hope for is obscurity, and that is a privilege they very rarely obtain.

Ignorant as they are in Europe of the inhabitants of the western states, they are fully as much so on the eastern side of this republic.   Although Kentucky has long filled the chair of Speaker in Congress, in a style which admits of no competition, and the office of clerk is retained by the unrivalled qualifications of another gentleman of that state; the Kentuckians in general are supposed by their fellow citizens of the east to be semibarbarians.

There is nothing that I anticipate with so

much satisfaction and security, as the rapid developement of society in our new country. Its
elements are rude certainly, and heterogeneous.
The first settlers, unprotected, and unassisted amid
dangers and difficulties, have been accustomed
from early youth to rely on their own powers ;
and they surrender with reluctance, and only by
halves, their right of defence against every aggression, even to the laws which themselves have constituted.

They have been anxiously studious of mildness in the forming of these laws, and when, in
practice, they seem inefficient, they too frequently
proceed with Indian perseverance to acts of
vengeance, inconsistent with the duty of forbearance essential to social man.   Hence deeds
of savage and even ferocious violence are too
common to be viewed with the abhorrence due to
them.

This disposition is evinced continually, and
acted on without any feeling of private or personal
animosity.

If a man, whom the public voice has proclaim-
ed a thief or a swindler, escapes from justice for
want of a legal proof of his guilt, though the law
and a jury of his fellow citizens have acquitted
him, ten to one but he is met with before he can
quit the neighbourhood, and, tied up to a sapling,

receives a scourging that marks him for the rest of his life.

In Kentucky, whose institutions have acquired greater maturity, such events *have* taken place some years ago; but now they would scarcely be tolerated, and they will soon be matter of history only, in Indiana and Illinois.

No crime but murder " of the first degree" is punished with death, in any of the western states, nor, I believe, in the Union. In Kentucky there is a general penitentiary, for the punishment of other offences by imprisonment and labour. A few weeks ago I read in the proceedings of that legislature, a report of a committee appointed to examine the state of this institution, by which it appears that only *forty-six individuals are in confinement*. How many of this number were committed during the last year I do not know, but I presume only a small proportion.

As this is the sole deposit of the criminals of a state containing probably half a million of inhabitants, (and a state where slavery is tolerated, though by no means universal) spread over a surface exceeding that of England and Wales,—where the laws being mild, are consequently executed with strictness, we must conclude that its institutions are wise and good, and favourable to morality.

The inhabitants of this western world will, and do afford a practical demonstration, that a well constituted society is not composed of governors by prescription, and a populace, or mob, their natural and proper subjects; but of men who have collected by delegation, in a common centre, the knowledge and power of the community to which they submit, as the only lawful government; all others being usurpations, whether administered by many or by few.

Our frontier position affords us many opportunities of obtaining information, which is highly interesting, on Indian manners and customs, from persons intimately acquainted with them by an intercourse of many years. Men who have fought with them and traded with them. A gentleman with whom I am in habits of frequent intercourse, a respectable neighbour of ours, has just returned from a trading expedition up the Red river, about seven hundred miles south-west of this place, among the Iotans, Cados, and Choctaws. He relates an event which occurred about Christmas last, at a place he visited, highly illustrative of the virtues and the vices of this untameable variety of the human family. Their simple necessaries of food and clothing are supplied as heretofore by the chase; but the skins of the various animals they kill have acquired, since their intercourse with the whites, a new value, and *they* have ac-

quired a taste for one fatal luxury, ardent spirits.
For these they barter their skins and furs. They
indulge in them to dreadful excess; and thousands
on thousands perish through intoxication, and the
frantic broils which it continually occasions. In
one of these frays a Cado bit off the under-lip of
a Choctaw, both young men; the latter was so
drunk, that he did not know who had been his an-
tagonist: he lost his lip, got sober, and returned
to the chase as usual. Some time after as he was
attending his beaver-traps with a comrade of his
own tribe, his companion divulged the secret, and
told the name of the Cado who had disfigured
him.

The Choctaw could not sustain the disgrace
when vengeance was practicable. He immediately
sold his whole property, his beaver-traps, his rifle,
and his horse; for these he obtained forty bottles
of whiskey. Thirty-nine bottles he consumed with
his friends, Iotans, Cados, and Choctaws, indifferently, in a grand debauch which lasted a w   ;
but reserved one bottle secreted for a special purpose. After this, when again sufficiently sober,
he joined a party, among whom was his devoted
foe—fell upon him with his knife, and dispatched
him. He then coolly took from his pouch some
red paint and smeared himself with it preparatory
to his death, which was a matter of course, as
blood must be avenged by blood, saying he should

be ready to die by ten o'clock the next day, but he wished to be shot by one of his own nation. The Cados were merciful; they told him he should not be shot by one of them, but by one of his own tribe, a friend of his own selection. He chose his friend, and he desired them to accompany him to a certain spot in the woods: they did so, and he directed them to dig a grave for him there. The next day he was missing: they sought for him at the appointed hour, and found him sitting at his grave, his bottle of whiskey by him. He drunk a part of it, and told them he was ready. His friend was also ready. He kept his seat, and holding up his arm, pointed to the place on his side where the ball should enter. The friend took aim—the gun missed fire: he gave a slight start, but said nothing. Again he raised his arm—again the gun snapped: he jumped up with some exclamation, took another draught of whiskey, and seated himself in the same place. The flint being chipped and all ready, once more he presented his side, and the fatal ball sent this brave man to an untimely grave.

Some time after they were talking over the melancholy affair, and the *friend* declared he was glad to shoot him, for he was not his friend in reality. The spirit of savage justice was roused again: one of his companions immediately fired

at him, but missed—thanks to the whiskey both
for the danger and the escape. However they
confined the *false friend* one whole week, whilst
they sat in council on the case. At length he was
acquitted of murder, and liberated, as he had only
taken a devoted life, though with the heart of a
traitor to his friend.

Since writing the above, I have found the
newspaper containing the account of the Kentucky penitentiary, and I give you a copy of the
statement as far as it relates to the employment of
the convicts :

In the cut nail manufactory	12
In the wrought nail ditto	7
Blacksmith's department	4
Shoe-makers	7
Chair-makers	5
Stone-cutting	6
Cooking and washing	2
Unfit for duty in consequence of disease	3
	46

Thus you see forty-six delinquents, of whom
forty-three are useful to the state.

In the same paper, " the Western Citizen,"
printed at Paris, Kentucky, Feb. 10, 1818, is another document, which I cannot forbear transcrib-
ing, because it shews that the citizens of Ken-

tuc ky are sensible that to be in the possession and exercise of the rights of self-government is a blessing ; and that their hearts are enlarged by it, and inflamed, not by jealousy of their neighbour's welfare, but with zeal to promote it.

Resolved by the General Assembly of the Commonwealth of Kentucky:

First: That the liberty of nations is derived from God and nature, and is not the gift of kings and potentates.

Second: That all just power is derived from the people, and the choice of forms of government belongs of right to them, and those (or their successors) who constitute a form may abrogate it.

Third: That in all just governments the good of the governed is the end to be accomplished; and the people upon whom each particular government operates are the only fit judges of the performance, to the ends for which the government was instituted.

Fourth: That the general revolt of a nation against oppression, and in vindication of their own liberty, cannot be justly called a rebellion.

Fifth: That the struggle of the patriots of South America for the right of self-government is justified by the laws of God and nature, and sanctified by the unalienable rights of man.

Sixth: That the success of those who are struggling for the liberty and independence of South America is a consummation devoutly to be wished, highly interesting to the friends of freedom and humanity in general, and calls for the deepest sympathy and accordance on the part of the people of the United States of North America.

Seventh: That it is the opinion of this General Assembly, that such of the provinces of South America as have declared themselves free and independent, and have shown reasonable ability to maintain their independence, ought forthwith to be acknowledged, by the general government of these United States of North America, sovereign and independent powers, to be treated as such, and introduced to the other sovereign powers of the earth: and generally, that all the rights of countenance and hospitality should be given by these United States to those so acknowledged sovereign powers of South America, which may, by the laws of nations, be justly and peaceably afforded by the people and magistracy of one neutral nation, to the people and magistracy of another nation, in war or in peace.

Resolved, That a copy of the foregoing resolutions be transmitted to the President of the United States, and to each of the senators and representatives of this state in the congress of the United States; and that the acting government be requested to transmit the above accordingly.

These resolutions are indicative of a good spirit, and thus are in accordance with the general feeling, as far as I can gather, of the citizens of all the states of the Union. You will not think highly of the composition: it has the prevailing fault of the American style, a redundancy of words; and it smells too strong of parchment.

It is extremely enlivening to perceive from our remote station, secluded as we seem from the busy theatre of life, that we have as good a view of what is passing, and are as warmly interested in the performance, as when we were seated in a side box at the very edge of the stage. In this wild spot I see my table strewed with newspapers, and registers, and reviews, in greater profusion than ever you saw it at Wanborough. We have daily papers from New York, and Philadelphia, at nine dollars a year; the National Intelligencer from Washington, three times a week, at six dollars; the weekly papers of the western country, at two dollars; Edinburgh and American Reviews, Monthly Magazines, Cobbett's Register, and

Niles's from Baltimore, &c. &c. Not a nerve is
touched in the remotest corner of the Union but
it vibrates in Washington, the *sensorium* of this
immense and truly living body. From this centre
of feeling intelligence, the impression is returned
to the extremities with a freshness that is as astonishing as it is delightful, through the unwearied
activity of an unshackled press. Thus we have
little solitude, or detachment from the great social
system, to complain of in our retirement. We
feel an interest, not at all diminished by our change
of position, in the commercial, and political, and
intellectual world; nay, for myself, if my sensi-
bility is not increased for what I conceive to be
the welfare of the great family, it is certainly more
pleasurable: it is a feeling of health and vigour,
instead of soreness and dejection. That my industry remains unimpaired, I prove to your full satisfaction by this immoderately long letter: of my
unabated regard and friendship you will need no
proof, whilst I can subscribe myself

unchangeably yours.

LETTER XXII.

MY DEAR SIR,   *March* 24, 1818.

I TRUST you have received several letters from me, although I have not yet had the pleasure of hearing from you since we parted. Those letters, and my printed journal, which I directed to be sent to you as soon as published, have made you of our party down to a very late period. You find that we are in a good country, are in no danger of perishing for want of society, and have abundant means of supplying every other want.

But I am sorry to inform you that our plan of colonising extensively, with a special view to the relief of our suffering countrymen of the lower orders, is not at present successful. A good number may be benefited by the arrangements we are making for their reception on a contracted scale; but the application to Congress, alluded to in my journal, which was calculated principally for the service of that class, has, I fear, proved abortive. I have transmitted to Congress, through

the hands of our member for Illinois, the following memorial:

To the Representatives of the United States in
Congress assembled, the Memorial of Morris
Birkbeck, an English farmer, lately settled in
the territory of Illinois, respectfully states—

That a number of his countrymen, chiefly
yeomen farmers, farming labourers, and rural
mechanics, are desirous of removing with their
families and their capital into this country, provided that, by having situations prepared for
them, they might escape the wearisome and expensive travel in quest of a settlement, which has
broken the spirits and drained the purses of many
of their emigrant brethren, terminating too frequently in disappointment.

Many estimable persons of the classes above
mentioned have reposed such a degree of confidence in the experience of your memorialist, as
would attract them to the spot which he has
chosen for himself. Their attention has accordingly been directed with some anxiety to his
movements; and when, after a laborious journey
through the states of Ohio and Indiana, he has
at length fixed on a situation in the Illinois
adapted to his private views, settlements are mul-

tiplying so rapidly around it, that it does not afford a scope of eligible unappropriated land, to which he could invite any considerable number of his friends.

There are, however, lands as yet unsurveyed lying about twenty miles north of this place, on which sufficient room might be obtained; and the object of this memorial is to solicit the grant by purchase of a tract of this land, for the purpose of introducing a colony of English farmers, labourers, and mechanics.

Feeling, as does your memorialist, that the people of England and the people of America are of one family, notwithstanding the unhappy political disputes which have divided the two countries, he believes that this recollection will be sufficient to insure, from the representatives of a free people, a favourable issue to his application in behalf of their suffering brethren.

(Signed)   MORRIS BIRKBECK.

Nov. 20, 1817.

My proposal in the above memorial was indefinite, designedly, that if acceded to, it might be on a general principle, to be extended as far as would be found beneficial; and might be guarded from abuse by provisions arising out of the principle itself. I entertained a hope that it would be referred to a committee, who would have permitted me to explain my views; and possibly I may yet have an opportunity of doing so, as I have not yet learned that it has been absolutely rejected. Other petitions for grants of land in favour of particular descriptions of emigrants have been rejected during this session, for reasons which my friends give me to understand will be fatal to mine. The following I consider to be the tenor of these objections:

That no public lands can be granted or disposed of but according to the general law on that subject, without a special act of legislation.

That although in certain cases such special acts have been made in favour of bodies of foreign emigrants, it has always been on the ground, and in consideration, of, a *general public* benefit accruing; such as the introduction of the culture of the vine by the Swiss colony at Vevay, Indiana, and the olive in Louisiana.

That it is not agreeable to the general policy of this government to encourage the settlement of foreigners in distinct masses, but rather to promote their speedy amalgamation with the community of American citizens.

And that all such grants are liable to be abused by speculators for private emolument.

Taking these objections in an inverted order, I think I could shew that the last would not apply to this case, where no indulgence is sought for in point of price. It would be sufficient for our purpose that certain lands, which are yet not surveyed, and of course unproductive, might be opened to us as an asylum, in which English emigrants *with* capital might provide for English emigrants *without* it. The title of these lands might remain in the United States until the purchase should be completed by actual settlers, paying the price on entry.

The nationality in some particulars which might be retained by such a settlement, would not surely be found to weigh against its usefulness.

When it is considered that the men with capital who emigrate as farmers are republicans to the core; that to such men, and the sons of such, the republic whose protection they now solicit, owes its existence—what is this nationality? is it not American in its essential qualities?

The poorer order of emigrants from England, what they have of politics is of the same cast; but the ignorance, the nullity, of a great proportion of the *rural* English population on these subjects, is wholly incomprehensible in this country.

Humanity, interest, necessity, will call for the

interference of the general government on behalf of those unfortunate persons who are cast destitute on the eastern shores, and on behalf of those cities and states which are burthened by them. But their countrymen, themselves citizens of the United States, or becoming so, would anticipate this interference, and crave permission to provide for them on some unappropriated spot, to which they would instantly give a value which it may not otherwise attain for ages.

That there is wanting the " *dignus vindice nodus ;*" that the object of this measure is not such as to warrant a solemn act of legislation ; that it is not of equal importance with the vineyards at Vevay, or the olive-grounds projected in Louisiana—when the several conditions of Great Britain, of the eastern states, and of this western country, are viewed in connexion with it—will hardly be maintained.

I have not the means of reference at hand, but I think it was about the year 1530 that the Portuguese brought from the old world the first cargo of muscles and sinews for the cultivation of the new. Nearly three hundred years has this dreadful export, with all that belongs to it, been sustained by Africa, until half America, with her islands, is peopled, not by freemen, but by overseers and slaves. If those muscles and sinews,

clothed as they were in sable, had come hither
animated by willing minds ; if the men who conducted, instead of staining themselves with atro-
cities which no pen can describe, had been employed in deeds of kindness ; if the masters who
received them had *paid* them for their labours instead of torturing them—but as all this was impossible, why *if* about the matter ?—That you may
for a moment glance over Africa, over the intervening ocean, and over that large portion of the
new world which Africa has peopled with un-
willing labourers, and think of the miseries and
the crimes that would have been spared to humanity during this period of three hundred years :
think what America and her islands would be
now, and how different their prospects, if involun-
tary servitude had never defiled her soil.

America yet needs muscles and sinews—Europe offers them.   They would come animated by
willing minds : deeds of kindness alone, costing
not a cent, are looked for from America.   If they
come in groups and remain so, they will be groups
of freemen.   Why does America love her government ?   Will not these men love it for the same
reason, and more intensely, from the recollection
of the bondage they have quitted ?

Thus I should talk to you were you here ; but
you are distant five thousand miles, and still I talk

to you.   Would that those who have most influence in this my adopted country could hear me
with the same mind that you will read this!

Adieu,

I am yours most truly.

P. S. I am just sending these letters to the
press, and I seize the occasion of dedicating them
to you.

TO

JOHN GALE, ESQ.

STERT, NEAR DEVIZES,

OLD ENGLAND.

THE END.